How to
G w Your Own Food

How to Grow Your Own Food

A week-by-week guide to wild life friendly fruit and vegetable gardening

Dirty Nails of *The Blackmore Vale Magazine*

SPRING HILL

Published by Spring Hill

Spring Hill is an imprint of
How To Books Ltd
Spring Hill House
Spring Hill Road
Begbroke
Oxford
OX5 1RX
Tel: (01865) 375794
Fax: (01865) 379162

info@howtobooks.co.uk
www.howtobooks.co.uk

First published 2007
Reprinted 2007
Reprinted 2008

British Library Cataloguing in Publication Data
A catalogue record of this book is available from the British Library

ISBN: 978-1-905862-11-5

Cover Design by Mousemat Design Ltd

Produced for How To Books by
Deer Park Productions, Tavistock
Designed and typeset by Mousemat Design Ltd
Printed and bound by Cromwell Press, Trowbridge, Wiltshire

Dirty Nails would like to
acknowledge the following
people who have been instru-
mental in helping to make the
dream of producing this book a
reality:

Fanny Charles and her staff at
the *Blackmore Vale Magazine*,
who have printed articles in
good faith every week since
February 2004.

Giles Lewis, Nikki Read and all
at How To Books, for their
generous help and support in
this venture.

Mrs Nails, for her unconditional
love and brilliant company.

CONTENTS

CONTENTS

FOREWORD

When the first Dirty Nails column landed on our news desk, we weren't sure what to do with it. Hand-written, in capital letters, and anonymous. Newspapers don't publish anonymous correspondence. But it had an air of authority. The slightly dog-eared paper looked authentic - this was someone who did get his (or her) hands dirty. We published it. The following week another column arrived. And so it went on, and we soon discovered there was a Mrs Nails. After a few months, we just expected its arrival, and our typesetter would ask, "Has Dirty Nails arrived?" He never missed a week. It seemed he never had a holiday.

Our long-established garden design columnist Pamela Bullmore thought she had found his plot, after she visited the allotments in Shaftesbury – she was sure it must be Dirty Nails because it was the only one growing salsify, and he had just written about this unusual vegetable. But we still didn't know who he was. Another contributor, Alison Shingler, of Gants Mill and Garden at Bruton, said she always read Dirty Nails. "Do you know who he is? He really knows his stuff," she said. "No," I said. "It just arrives each week, hand-written, and we publish it." Alison laughed. "Only the *Blackmore Vale Magazine* could have an anonymous gardening correspondent," she said.

We are delighted and proud that our Dirty Nails can take his recipe for wildlife friendly gardening to a nationwide audience.

Fanny Charles
Editor, *Blackmore Vale Magazine*

PREFACE

Everyone, regardless of background, status or class ultimately depends on the land for their food and survival.

It is this basic instinctive need that first inspired Dirty Nails to start growing food crops. His efforts have nothing to do with cultivating the largest, roundest, shiniest onion or longest, straightest runner bean. Such pastimes are for others. His passion is simply for eating good honest food, following the natural order of things on the plot, tuning in to the ebb and flow of life beyond computer screens and outside of walls and windows. For Dirty Nails, to feel the sun on his back or rain in his face, to cut a lettuce in midsummer or gather lovingly tended produce for a deep-winter feast in icy conditions with freezing hands and fingers red raw, that is the stuff of dreams. To be at one with the elements, to have a place in the never ending cycle of life death and rebirth, to commune with the amazing diversity of plants and creatures that come and go with the changing seasons as he does, these are the magical ingredients which combine to make his gardening experience such an exquisite one.

It is the almost child-like love of what he does and where he is that first inspired Dirty Nails to put pen to paper and record day-to-day life in the garden. From these scribbled notes, reminders and observations to himself came a weekly article in the *Blackmore Vale Magazine*. Out of a desire to reach an audience beyond the confines of Dorset and Somerset came this book. His wish is that it will help you to grow your own food and have the time of your life whilst doing it!

For Dirty Nails

LEEKS

Now is the time to start thinking about your leeks. Dirty Nails likes to get his autumn leeks on the go as early as possible. To this end he will be sowing seeds of an autumn variety in trays this week. Carentan 2 is an ideal variety.

Sow the small black seeds thinly in a tray of potting compost and cover lightly. These will do well if kept moist, and set on a windowsill indoors until the grass-like shoots appear. It won't take too many days.

It is always a thrill when the first leeks start sprouting. The trays can go into the greenhouse at this stage, and then be planted out into a nursery bed from about the end of March.

Dirty Nails always over-does it with his leeks. But this is good, because half the crop can be dug up and eaten for a sweet tasting baby leek treat around the middle of July.

NATURAL HISTORY IN THE GARDEN
Badgers in February

Badgers that live close by will be giving birth at this time of year. Two or three cubs per female are usual. They spend the first eight weeks or so in their underground breeding chamber, which will be lined with soft, dried vegetation that the badgers collect from around and about. When they are cleaning out these chambers, or bringing in fresh bedding, debris is often left scattered in the vicinity of their hole, or sett. Such evidence of badgers is particularly noticeable this month.

VEGETABLE SNIPPETS

A BRIEF HISTORY OF
THE LEEK

The leek, *Allium porrum*, occurs naturally across a region that stretches all the way from Israel to India, and has been cultivated as an important food source since at least 3500 BC. Its distribution throughout Europe was assured by the Ancient Egyptians, Greeks and Romans. The latter, who brought leeks to Britain after AD 43, knew leeks as *porrum*. After their Empire collapsed in AD 410 this crop, along with cabbages (brassicas) and beans (pulses), became an important dietary ingredient throughout the British and European Dark Ages. In Saxon times leeks were widely grown, and the Anglo-Saxon term laec tun, which actually means leek enclosure, can be found today in both family and place names, including Layton, Leighton, Latham, Lighton and Letton.

Leeks were exported to the so-called New World. By 1775 both settlers and Native Americans were raising leeks for the pot in what was to become the United States. Back in the UK this member of the onion tribe remained popular through the Little Ice Age that took place between the sixteenth and nineteenth centuries, when it was happily able to withstand the drop in temperatures as a 'standing crop' (left in the fields and dug as required in winter).

Often overlooked in more recent times, leeks offer a gourmet meal when cooked gently until tender. The French, notorious as connoisseurs of fine foods, are apt to compare a well prepared dish of leeks with that much sought-after delicacy, asparagus.

PATHS

The wet weather of late has put the kibosh on digging and ground preparation this week. Instead, Dirty Nails has turned his attention to paths in the vegetable garden. Wooden planks are all very well for temporary access to crops, but where regular routes are walked Dirty Nails suggests something more solid.

He likes to construct his paths with old bricks and gathers them wherever he can from skips and dumps. Only unbroken ones will do. Lay them side-by-side across, and set them out as the path will go. Then simply use a spade to dig out two-thirds the depth of the brick, and break up the bottom of the trench. Move the bricks to one side as you do this, and place them back in as you progress with a half-inch (1¼ cm) or so between them. They will settle comfortably in the trench with a stamp of a foot. The spade can be employed to scatter some of the excavated soil onto the bricks, and a piece of wood used to scrape this into the cracks. Then ram it down with a thin edge. Finally, sweep clean.

The structure these paths give to the garden is very pleasing, and they instantly blend in with a look of natural permanence. Walk and wheel-barrow as much as you like, as this all helps the bricks to nestle in. A path constructed thus can be left for years, or shifted with a minimum of fuss and disruption as the garden evolves.

NATURAL HISTORY IN THE GARDEN
Wild Arum

Lush, deep green whorls of leaves are popping up in the wild garden edges. They belong to the wild arum, which is also known as cuckoo pint, or lords and ladies. This is a fascinating wild flower with a very unusual way of reproducing. From the centre it sends up a smelly brown spike which attracts insects. These are captured by the plant and held hostage overnight by one-way, hair-like triggers. When pollination via the insects has occurred the triggers wither, and the captives are released unharmed. All this excitement happens in April and May. For now, the fresh bundles of growth are just a promise of the natural magic to come.

VEGETABLE SNIPPETS

LIVING WITH
TRAVELLING BADGERS

Paths should be constructed so as to allow comfortable wheelbarrow access. Making them too narrow will result in awkward manoeuvring of this essential piece of kit. When crops are in the ground, especially once well into the growing season, they can flop over a narrow path. This not only causes damp trouser bottoms in wet weather, but also potentially damages the crop itself through bruising as the gardener brushes past. A nice, wide path is a pleasure, one that is tight a pain.

Creating regularly used and well-worn routes is not a condition restricted just to humans. Badgers and deer are creatures of habit, and if they are resident in the area of the veg plot evidence of their night-time wanderings will be conspicuous. Badgers are apt to use the same paths from homes to foraging sites over generations. A patch or scrape of bare soil under a fence is telltale, and the discovery of coarse white-tipped black and white hairs caught on thorns or barbed wire hereabouts is even stronger evidence of them passing to and fro. It is very difficult to dissuade badgers from using their favourite paths, and blocking their way can prove both frustrating (to the gardener) and damaging (to the fence).

Dirty Nails recommends that a sturdy two-way gate be installed in this situation. It works along the lines of a small dog-sized cat flap. Alternatively, a gap can be left which will allow these handsome nocturnal beasts free passage as they like.

BEAN TRENCHES AND LETTUCE

February, 3rd Week

Bean Trenches

Dirty Nails has just finished filling the second of his runner bean trenches with compostable kitchen waste. Trodden down, then covered with the excavated soil, the decomposing waste will ensure plenty of goodness for this summer's runners. He has dug his trenches along a shed and fence that receive plenty of sun, because he likes to grow his runners as an edible screen.

Trench-composting consists of digging a ditch one spit deep (depth of a spade head) and filling it with rottable refuse. Discarded vegetable matter can be added bit by bit over time, and will break down slowly. When the trench is full, cover over with soil. Locked-up goodness is gradually released below the soil surface in the 'root zone'. This is exactly where crops, including hungry beans, want nourishment most. Runner bean seedlings will eventually be planted outside in mid-May at 8 inch (20 cm) intervals, so the trench must be dug to the desired length according to the number of individuals that are to be grown.

Well-rotted farmyard manure (FYM) can also be used for this method of feeding veggies. It is a superb alternative to the contents of the compost bucket, but can be a little harder to come by these days.

Lettuce

In the greenhouse, or indoors, Dirty Nails has been sowing lettuces. Iceberg Talia, or Lobjoits Green Cos, are ideal for sowing now in trays of moist compost. As soon as the second pair of true leaves are forming he

NATURAL HISTORY IN THE GARDEN
Woodpeckers

Woodpeckers are making a noise this month. They will be busy in surrounding big trees, communicating with each other. Both the greater and lesser spotted varieties use trees as sounding boards. The greater has distinctive red feathers at the base of its tail, and is both bigger and more common than the blackbird-sized lesser. The drumming noise is made by rapid blows of their beaks on branches, and up to ten drums can occur per second. Greater spotted 'peckers have a deep repeat which fades at the end. The lesser is higher pitched and stops abruptly.

gets them out into the sunniest spot possible. Dirty Nails pegs plastic bells over his first outdoor lettuces, which brings them on a treat. With a bit of luck these lettuces will be ready for cutting and eating by late April or early May. This is one of those early-season moments that makes life worth living.

VEGETABLE SNIPPETS
A LOOK AT
THE LETTUCE

Lactuca serriola still grows all over Europe, North Africa and the temperate parts of Asia. This plant is the wild predecessor of all the multitude of different types of cultivated lettuce. In Britain it is commonly known as prickly lettuce. The Ancient Egyptians are believed to have been the first to begin domesticating this plant, and it was extremely popular by Roman times. Known in those days as vinegar salads, lettuces were served as a first course at banquets, and eaten with great gusto on account of the supposed aphrodisiac qualities contained within the leaves. By the fourteenth century lettuces were being widely cultivated in Britain.

As well as being nutritionally useful sources of vitamins A, C and B9 (folic acid), potassium and iron, lettuces also contain small amounts of a narcotic not dissimilar to opium. It is this which has earned these leafy saladings their reputation for aiding restful sleep. In Beatrix Potter's story *The Tale of the Flopsy Bunnies* the rabbits who raided Mr McGregor's vegetable patch succumbed to these soporific qualities.

JERUSALEM ARTICHOKES

February, 4th Week

Dirty Nails likes to get his Jerusalem artichokes into the ground as soon as it is workable in the New Year, but any time until mid-March will suffice. He plants his at the back of the veg patch, in a line that won't cast shade on other crops. Jerusalem artichokes are very dense of growth, and thus ideal for screening off unsightly compost heaps or fences.

Dirty Nails incorporates leaf-mould and grass clippings by digging them into the soil. He plants his artichokes, saved from a previous crop or simply bought from the grocers, 1 foot (30 cm) apart and 5 inches (12½ cm) deep. This root vegetable will grow in the poorest conditions, but a little tender loving care will repay with a fine crop of knobbly tubers.

All the plants need is to be kept watered and weed-free. Earth-up around the base when there is about a foot of growth. Cut off a third of the tops after mid-summer, to prevent wind-rock. At the end of August Dirty Nails always reduces the top growth by half.

Harvesting can commence any time from November. One plant is dug at a time, and the bounty stored in boxes of damp sand until needed. Ten plants should keep a family of four comfortably supplied all winter.

NATURAL HISTORY IN THE GARDEN
Song Thrush

Listen out for the song thrush enriching an otherwise dull February landscape. They like to perch high up in big lime trees. Their early morning song is a repetitive series of beautiful, tuneful, fluting, liquid notes and elaborate musical clicks and whistles, punctuated by short, well-timed pauses. The speckle-breasted birds open their beaks widely and constantly turn their heads whilst delivering this chorus, providing a musical treat for the listener.

VEGETABLE SNIPPETS
JERUSALEM ARTICHOKES
DEMYSTIFIED

The Jerusalem artichoke (*Helianthus tuberosus*) is neither from Jerusalem, nor an artichoke. In fact this vegetable heralds from North America. It was a staple foodstuff for Native Americans from Nova Scotia in the east to Minnesota and Kansas, well before Columbus 'discovered' the continent.

'Jerusalem' is believed to be a corruption of *girasola*, which in Italian means 'turning towards the sun'. This refers to the habit of the pretty yellow flowers, about 2½ inches (6 cm) in diameter, which like to open into the sun. Its true family is thus revealed: the Jerusalem artichoke is in fact a tuberous-rooted relation of the sunflower.

Nutritionally high in iron, potassium, and thiamine, and alternatively known as the sunchoke, or sun root, the Jerusalem was being marketed in Europe by the early 1600s. At that time it was called the Canada, or French, potato. It was also introduced to Britain around then, along with such delicacies as cultivated strawberries, different beans, gourds, sweet peppers and tomatoes.

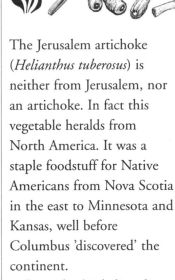

BROAD BEANS

Dirty Nails has planted out his broad beans this week. The productive and very early Witkeim variety is his choice for sowing at this time of year.

The large, browny-grey seeds feel substantial in his hand, and Dirty Nails loves planting them. He places the magical pieces on the surface of the evenly raked soil in a line at 5 inch (12 cm) intervals. If he sows a double row, then he allows 8 inches (20 cm) between lines.

When he has set his seeds out as desired, he gently presses them into the soil end-on to a depth of 2 inches (5 cm), and covers them over. If it is cold Dirty Nails puts cloches over the top to keep the seedbed warmer.

Home-grown broad beans really do taste completely different to shop-bought, and are highly nutritious. With luck, a sowing this week will be producing pods of fat beans around mid-summer.

NATURAL HISTORY IN THE GARDEN
Pied Wagtails

Small black and white birds with long black flicking-up tails and a low, undulating, dancy flight, are pied wagtails. They gather on the lawn in ones and twos, sometimes more. The pied wagtail bobs its head back and fore as it quarters the ground with rapid darting runs, occasionally jumping up acrobatically to snaffle low flying insects.

VEGETABLE SNIPPETS

SOME FACTS ABOUT
THE BROAD BEAN

Scientifically, the broad bean is *Vicia faba*, also known as the fava bean. Horse bean or field bean are other alternatives, although these last two names generally refer to crops that are commonly grown as animal fodder. Broads popular for human consumption nowadays are larger-seeded varieties. Native to North Africa and Southwest Asia, these beans are believed to have been part of the European diet even before 6000 BC. They were particularly popular in the Stone Age Mediterranean region. European folklore has it that planting this crop either on Good Friday or at night-time is a harbinger of good luck.

Broad beans are rich in protein, so much so that they have been called 'vegetable meat'. Vitamins A and C are readily available, so too phosphorous. Broads contain the cancer fighting substance lectin, so may help in this department also.

PARSNIPS

Parsnips can be sown any time from mid-February until the end of April. Dirty Nails has planted his first sowing in the ground this week. 'Snips prefer a deeply dug bed raked into a fine tilth, with as few stones as possible. White King is a variety which can produce large tender roots in these conditions. If your soil is rather shallow and/or stony, try Avonresister.

Having prepared the ground, mark out your rows, each one a foot (30 cm) apart. Dirty Nails likes to station-sow his parsnips at 6 inch (15 cm) intervals. This is a simple task which involves pushing a finger into the soil to a depth of ¾ inch (2 cm). Place three of the confetti-like seeds into each shallow hole, cover, and firm gently. Choose a dry, calm day for this, as even a slight breeze can cause the seeds to become very hard to handle. When Dirty Nails

NATURAL HISTORY IN THE GARDEN
Daisies and Dandelions

The old saying goes that spring is truly sprung when a maiden can put her foot on seven daisies. That is sure to be the case in the days ahead on the lawn, as these lovely little flowers start to really get going, popping up their cheery heads all over the place. The name daisy comes from 'day's eye', which sums up this low growing plant perfectly. In the bright sunshine they spread their petals to catch the rays, but close them up when it is dull and overcast.

Dandelions have been showing themselves shyly for a few weeks now, but they will be producing their sun-like yellow flower heads in profusion soon. These beautiful, bold flowers would surely be cherished more if they were not so common. They are especially valuable to bees and hoverflies that are on the wing in early spring.

sows his Avonresister later this month, he will halve the planting distance because the roots are smaller.

Like most veg 'snips like to be kept moist and weed-free. They are slow germinators, and it may be over a month before the seedlings emerge from the soil. Be patient! Thin to the strongest seedling, and enjoy the wait. Roasted parsnip is a highlight of the long winter months.

VEGETABLE SNIPPETS
A BRIEF HISTORY OF
THE PARSNIP

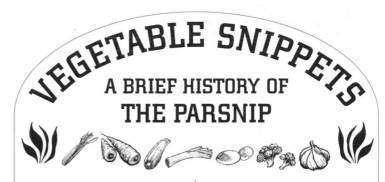

Wild parsnip (*Pastinaca saliva*) grows all over Britain on well drained grasslands and waste ground. It is most at home on alkaline chalky and limestone soils. Above ground, the flowers and foliage of the wild version are very similar to its well-bred, domesticated cousin. Indeed, biologically they are the same plant. However, selective breeding down the generations has differentiated them, and developed the fat root in one which is so popular in the kitchen.

Parsnips are native throughout Eurasia and have been eaten since ancient times. In fact until the sixteenth century, when potatoes arrived in Britain from the Americas, they were a staple part of the winter diet. Parsnips are rich in dietary fibre as well as numerous vitamins and minerals, especially potassium and calcium. It is exposure to cold temperatures which prompts starch in the root to become sugar. This desirable sweetness is the main reason why the advice traditionally is not to lift 'snips until after the first frost.

ONIONS

Planting onion sets is an early spring highlight for Dirty Nails, especially if he has warm morning sunshine on his back when doing so. The job has been completed this week. The onion bed was thoroughly prepared beforehand, with leaf-mould and well rotted manure dug in, then wood ash raked in. Dirty Nails likes to give his onion bed two or three good rakings before he treads it all down. Onions like a firm footing. Stuttgarter Giant, Sturon and Red Baron are all widely available as sets.

Dirty Nails marks out his rows a foot (30 cm)

NATURAL HISTORY IN THE GARDEN
Badgers in March

The breeding period for badgers gets into full swing in March, April and May, and continues until the autumn. However the females (sows) can hold fertilised eggs in their bodies in a kind of suspended animation, known as delayed implanta-tion, until December. The embryonic badgers are then allowed to develop, and are born around mid-January to mid-March. They enter the world virtually bald, and will remain blind for the first five weeks of their lives.

VEGETABLE SNIPPETS
SOME FACTS ABOUT ONIONS

The Ancient Egyptians held that onions symbolised eternal life. This is thought to be on account of this bulbous vegetable's globular shape and the concentric rings concealed within its papery skin. Cultivation is believed to have commenced in that part of the world around 3000 BC and onions are one of the first domesticated crops ever to be written about.

Cultivated onions (*Allium cepa*) are just one of about 450 species in the allium family known about worldwide. Many, though by no means all, are edible. These days raising a harvest from sets, as opposed to seed, is considered to be a consistently reliable method of producing food in the kitchen garden or on the allotment. Sets are simply small onions, part-grown and then heat treated. Fewer varieties are available commercially compared to seeds, and this does limit choice for the gardener. They are also a more expensive way of growing this veg although in truth it is only a matter of pennies. However the flip-side of this is that mass produced sets have democratised onion growing, giving everyone the opportunity to be successful in nurturing a good crop of onions.

apart, and places the acorn-sized onions along these rows at 6 inch (15 cm) intervals. When they are in place it is simply a case of pushing each tiny onion into the soil, leaving just the husky tip standing proud. Use a finger to make a little nest for each one, and firm it in. Keep an eye on them closely for the first week or so and press back any that are lifted by frost, birds, or their own sprouting roots. Keep moist and weed-free, watch the green shoots grow, and the bulbs swell. It will be well into August before Dirty Nails thinks about harvesting.

RADISHES

March, 4th Week

Dirty Nails has been sowing seeds this week, direct into the soil. Quick growing French Breakfast radish is a favourite, and will be sown every ten days or so in short lines to ensure a summer-long supply of chunky, peppery roots. The drills only need to be less than an inch (2½ cm) deep, and can be grooved out of a level raked bed using a trowel edge or with fingers. Radish seeds are large enough to handle individually. Dirty Nails carefully places these in the bottom of his drill at 2 inch (5 cm) intervals, and brushes soil over the top of them with the back of his hand. He gently firms, or 'tamps', the covered drill with the back of a rake, and waters with the rose on his can. Radishes are thirsty veg and like to be grown in soil kept moist.

The French Breakfast variety is prolific. Sown individually, thinning is kept to a minimum, and therefore so too is wastage. Dirty Nails pulls his radishes when they are showing their bright red shoulders proud out of the soil and are approximately 2 inches (5 cm) in cylindrical length, which should be in a few short weeks.

NATURAL HISTORY IN THE GARDEN
Jackdaws

Look out for members of the crow family congregating in numbers this month. A dozen or more jackdaws may hang out in tall trees overlooking the garden, watching keenly for a feeding opportunity. These handsome black and grey fellows are highly intelligent, sociable creatures. When one jack' sees the coast clear to land and have a poke about, it will soon be joined by others. They eat whatever they can find in the way of kitchen scraps, seeds, fruit, insects, carrion, and other birds' eggs and nestlings in season.

VEGETABLE SNIPPETS

A RUNDOWN ON
RADISHES

Radishes (*Raphanus sativus*) are related to cabbages. Therefore, although a quick and easy crop to grow, they should be spared from sowing on ground either side of cultivating kale, purple sprouting broccoli, Brussels sprouts and the like. This is in order to allow the soil time to recover fertility, and break the life cycle of any of the many pests and diseases which are prone to afflict this family of foodstuffs. Having said that, radishes are otherwise generally very rewarding, with predation by slugs and snails the only major problem that Dirty Nails has encountered with them.

The first domesticated radishes are believed to have originated in China many moons ago. French Breakfast is an old heirloom variety which has been widely grown since the late 1800s on account of the beautiful looking, peppery tasting, red and white roots. Nutritionally high in potassium and vitamin C, radishes are wont to bolt (flower and set seed) in dry conditions. If this happens the young seed pods can be pinched off and eaten as a tasty nibble.

GLOBE ARTICHOKES

March, 5th Week

Globe artichokes are considered a luxury in some circles, but their exquisite taste and fascinating growth make them an essential part of Dirty Nails' veg plot. This edible thistle is generally easy to grow, and if space is tight they will be quite happy at the back of the flower border too.

Dirty Nails has been in the greenhouse this week sowing seeds of the Green Globe variety. Bluish-grey and the size of a sunflower seed, they are simply nestled into potting compost ½ inch (1½ cm) down. Around mid-summer the young plants should be ready for planting out. In subsequent years, when big bud production is in full swing, globe artichokes will make a bushy clump of coarse, silvery-green leaves which like space, moisture and sunshine, so give them plenty of room to grow. Three feet (1 metre) may seem excessive when less than a year old, but your rewards will come.

In the year after sowing, Dirty Nails harvests only the main, or 'king', bud. He pinches the smaller buds out before they come to anything. In subsequent years each plant may produce over half a dozen buds the size of a fist. These are cut, with a portion of stem attached, from June to October before the globes begin to open. Boiled until tender, there is a mouthful of artichoke flesh to be scraped from the bottom of each bud 'leaf', and a gorgeous 'heart' within to be savoured. The hairy 'choke', however, must be avoided.

Dirty Nails ensures a succession of plants that are at their peak by sowing a few seeds each year, and by knifing-away side growths with some root attached from strong plants in their three or four year-old

NATURAL HISTORY IN THE GARDEN
Brimstone Butterfly

A warm spell this month will tempt the first butterflies out of hibernation. Keep an eye out for the brimstone, which over-winters in its adult form under loose bark, in thick ivy, or other frost-free hidey-holes. Its lovely plain yellow colouration, slightly paler on females, is what puts the 'butter' into butterfly.

prime. These suckers, taken in autumn or spring, are replanted and treated as one year-olds.

VEGETABLE SNIPPETS
A BRIEF HISTORY OF
GLOBE ARTICHOKE

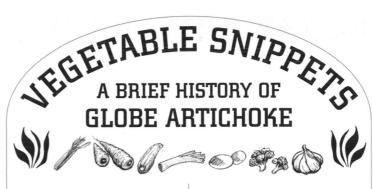

It is thought that globe artichokes originated in the Mediterranean. There is evidence that this plant was being cultivated for food in Italy and Sicily from about 300 BC. The Greeks and Romans are credited with exporting globes further afield. The fact that *Cynara scolymus*, as it is known scientifically, does best when afforded a sizeable plot to grow in and produces a relatively small return for this space, meant that at this time it was homed mainly in the aristocratic gardens of Europe. Here globe artichokes achieved gourmet status and were highly prized on account of their reputed aphrodisiac and breath-freshening qualities. Globes were introduced to Britain in the sixteenth century.

Considered by many to be a luxury vegetable, these artichokes are nutritionally rich in vitamin C, folic acid, potassium and dietary fibre. Green Globe is one of the most popular of many varieties available today and hails from America.

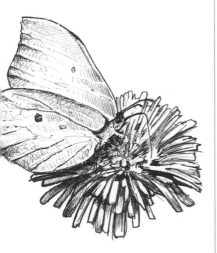

SCORZONERA, SALSIFY AND CALENDULA

Scorzonera

Dirty Nails has been digging, raking and sowing in the veg plot this week. Scorzonera is an ancient vegetable, and a particular favourite of his which can be planted at any time from now until mid-May. The black, thong-like root may penetrate so deep that digging it out in one piece becomes a personal challenge. It is delicious eaten raw, steamed or baked.

Because of the length of root Dirty Nails sows his scorzonera in a deeply dug bed which is as stone-free as possible. The seeds resemble large grains of rice and are sown at 6 inch (15 cm) intervals, 1½ inches (4 cm) deep. Dirty Nails sows two seeds at a time and thins to the strongest seedling as soon as the grass-like shoots have arched out of the soil. Scorzonera is simple to grow. All it demands is to be kept moist and weed free. It will stand happily in the ground all winter for digging out as and when required.

Salsify

Salsify is a root veg that resembles a large white carrot. Dirty Nails grows it in exactly the same way as for scorzonera. It has a delectable flavour and is well worth growing. Two or three 10 foot (3 metre) lines of both salsify and scorzonera should be ample for even the hungriest family of four.

Calendula

Dirty Nails has also been sowing calendula (pot

NATURAL HISTORY IN THE GARDEN
Ornamental Purple Plum and Small Tortoiseshell Butterfly

Ornamental purple plum

Ornamental purple plum trees are at their peak early in the month. Delicate pale pink blossom feathers the branches like a dusting of rose-tinted snow. They give way to dark maroon leaves, and the show is over.

The small tortoiseshell butterfly

All manner of insects will be on the wing. A commonly observed butterfly is the small tortoiseshell. It has orange and dark brown wings, bordered on the back-facing edge with eye-catching half moons. They will be laying eggs on the underside of nettle leaves as May approaches, which will hopefully lead to a new small tortoiseshell generation around midsummer. Fine weather is often the order of the day if butterflies are visible doing their rounds before nine o'clock in the morning.

April, 1st Week

marigold) around the outside of his veg plot this week. There seems to be something about calendula that inhibits tenacious weeds like couch grass, and it is for this weed control purpose that he grows it in this way. It is dead easy. Scatter the seeds as required and cover with a fine layer of soil. The resulting riot of orange and yellow flowers creates a glorious bee and insect-rich arena for the vegetables growing within.

VEGETABLE SNIPPETS

SALSIFY IN THE WILD AND SOME SCORZONERA FACTS

Salsify

Salsify grows wild in Britain as *Trapogon pratensis*, commonly known as Jack-go-to-bed-at-noon. This descriptive name refers to the yellow daisy-like flower. It is borne on a slender, grass-like stalk, opens early in the morning throughout high-summer and closes by noon. It sets seed by forming a 'clock' similar to a dandelion, only bigger and with chunkier seeds. They are spread via the wind, carried away with the aid of a parachute comprising a disc of feathery hairs.

In olden days the root of this plant was boiled in milk and given as a tonic to folk who were recovering from illness. The cultivated salsify differs only in that the delicate bloom is purple.

Scorzonera

Scorzonera (*Scorzonera hispanica*) heralds from Southern Europe and the Near East. Its widespread status can be attributed to the Spanish who exported this impressive root vegetable far and wide. The name scorzonera comes from Old French, which was the spoken language a thousand years ago of northern France, Belgium and Switzerland. It means snake. The long, black tap root is indeed serpent-like, and traditionally this plant was used to treat snake bites. Other names include black oyster plant, Spanish salsify, serpent root, viper's grass.

Scorzonera is a member of the family of flowers which includes the aster and is frequently represented in gardens by the Michaelmas daisy. It is also a favourite food-plant of a common resident moth known as the nutmeg (*Discestra trifolii*). The adults of this insect are superficially just earthy-brown in colour, but close inspection reveals a wonderful array of patterns and marbling. There are generally two generations on the wing in the south, in early summer and early autumn, with a mid-summer performance north of the Midlands. Night-flying adults are attracted to nectar-rich flowers, sugar and light. As juveniles the larvae are called clover cutworms. Later broods will over-winter in the topsoil, within a delicate chrysalis. These may be turned up whilst harvesting scorzonera roots throughout winter.

LEEKS AND LETTUCES

Leeks

This week Dirty Nails has been planting his baby autumn leeks (Carentan 2), which were sown indoors during February, outside into a nursery bed. For this, soil has been raked to a fine tilth, and then made moist. Use a rose-ended watering can or sprinkler hose if the soil is dry. Rows are then marked out with canes and string, to a desired length, 6 inches (15 cm) apart. Dirty Nails makes holes along each row with a pencil, bamboo cane or straight twig, at 3 inch (8 cm) intervals and 2 inches (5 cm) deep.

The leeks, which each look like a thin strand of grass, will have a couple or three long, trailing roots. They need to be eased gently out of their seed tray and carefully teased apart. Extra-long roots can be trimmed by a half with no ill effects. They are placed individually into the holes, making sure the roots are as nestled down as possible and not poking out of the top. They are then 'puddled in', which means that they are watered directly in their holes. Soil will fall naturally over the roots and should be nicely bedded in after a few such puddlings. When they have grown to pencil thickness after mid-summer, they will be ready to go into the leek bed proper, or eaten as they are, young and sweet.

Lettuces

Greenhouse-grown lettuces

NATURAL HISTORY IN THE GARDEN
Badgers in April

Badgers are very active this month. Young cubs born in February, now fully furred and with eyes wide open, will be tempted to have a peek out from the mouth of their sett entrance and sniff the air above ground. If family groups are crowded, fighting can occur at this time of year. Last season's boars (males), who are low down in the pecking order, may be driven out. It is a noisy affair, with vicious squabbling sometimes leading to nasty injuries, especially under the rump. Displaced badgers will have to make their own way in the world from now on. These brutal encounters can sound prehistoric as they scrap, roll and tumble in the darkness amongst the brambles and undergrowth.

VEGETABLE SNIPPETS
LETTUCE CHAT

such as Lobjoits Green Cos, Talia and Buttercrunch, which were sown in the latter part of February, are ready to be planted outside now. Dirty Nails places plastic bells over his transplanted lettuces to keep them growing fast when the weather can still be a bit nippy. Lettuces need about 8 inches (20 cm) between plants, and like to be kept sunny and moist. Salad days will soon be here, especially if the odd juicy leaf is taken early.

Lettuces are the food plant for numerous species of moth whose grub-like larvae are collectively known as cutworms. They are considered by some to be damaging, although Dirty Nails is not of this opinion. He prefers to view cutworms as a valuable part of the garden ecology. As adults, the moths are lovely. Those for whom lettuces are enjoyed in early life include the large yellow underwing, the garden dart, the common swift and the angle shades. The latter is common throughout Britain

and, despite the fact that it over-winters as a chrysalis just below the soil surface, adults may be seen on the wing during any month of the year.

Cos lettuces form crisp heads of elongated leaves, and are also known as Romaine lettuces.

Iceberg lettuces are also called crisphead lettuces. Their dense, round heads do not look unlike a cabbage. Home-grown icebergs are a pleasure and treat to eat with their wonderful crunchy texture and distinctive, cooling flavour.

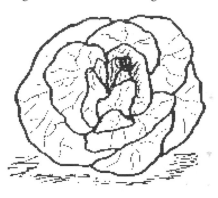

BEETROOT AND COURGETTES

April, 3rd Week

Beetroot

This is the perfect time to start sowing beetroot, and Dirty Nails has been doing just that this week. He likes to sow the Detroit 2 variety and puts down a 6 foot (2 metre) line every fortnight from now until July. Hopefully this will ensure a steady supply of golfball-sized, sweet-yet-earthy roots from midsummer and through the autumn. In June and July he also sows the long-rooted Cylindra. This variety has an extra intense flavour and a beautiful texture when boiled until tender.

Beetroot seeds are small and knobbly. They should be sown thinly not more than an inch (2½ cm) deep. Dirty Nails allows 12 inches (30 cm) between each line. Germination can be anything from a few days to a fortnight or so, depending on the weather. Detroit 2 and Cylindra seeds are multi-germ, which means that each one may produce two, three or four seedlings. These should be thinned to the strongest as soon as they are big enough to handle. Dirty Nails aims to thin his beets to 5 inch (13 cm) intervals in order to allow each one room to grow. As always, beets like to be kept moist and weed-free.

Courgettes

Dirty Nails sows his courgettes around now, in the greenhouse or on a windowsill. He pops the large, flat, oval seeds on edge into 3 inch (7½ cm) pots full of potting compost, an inch (2½ cm) deep. Kept moist, they should grow on nicely,

NATURAL HISTORY IN THE GARDEN
Cuckoo arrival

April is the month for keeping an early morning or evening ear out for the cuckoo. These birds return to Britain from Africa in the late spring to breed, and will hopefully be arriving around the 15th. Males sing the unmistakable 'cu-coo' which is so evocative of England as summer beckons. The female has a completely different call, a water-bubbling chuckle. For now, cuckoos will be focusing on recovering from their long overseas migration, feeding up and finding a mate.

and will be gradually hardened off prior to planting out in May (this simply involves putting them outside in the daytime, and bringing indoors at night). Deep-green Black Beauty or yellow Goldrush are prolific, and the speedy growth of a courgette can be truly amazing. They are best picked small and are lovely grated raw, stir-fried or lightly steamed.

VEGETABLE SNIPPETS
A BRIEF HISTORY OF
THE BEETROOT

The beetroot is one of many gastronomically important vegetables descended from *Beta vulgaris*, also known as the sea-beet, which is native to western and southern European coastlines from Sweden to the Mediterranean. This is believed to include Britain, although it is not until 1629 that the sea-beet is recorded in England. Selective breeding in the 1500s produced the familiar swollen-rooted crop, and by the 1700s beetroot was popular fare at European mealtimes.

Full of natural sugars, beetroots are sweeter than the average vegetable. Their consumption is thought to promote relaxation and a general sense of well-being. In recent years supposed aphrodisiac qualities have been much vaulted.

HOEING, ROOT VEG AND RUNNER BEANS

Hoeing

A dry spell at this time of year means perfect hoeing weather. Dirty Nails gets busy with his hoe as early in the day as possible, to give sunshine plenty of time to shrivel up the annihilated weeds. He aims to pass the blade back and forth through the top layer of soil with small, smooth strokes. Dirty Nails keeps his blade sharp with a small file which he carries in his pocket. Stopping regularly to keep his blade keen also allows him an opportunity to stretch his back. The hoe is number one tool in the battle with weeds from now on and through the summer. He loves getting in amongst his crops, having a really close look all the time. Hoe when it is sunny, dry and before you can see the weeds.

Runner Beans

Runner beans can be sown now. Dirty Nails grows Enorma, which is high yielding with long, straight beans of excellent flavour. He also grows White Emergo which is an old-fashioned, white flowered variety. It is prolific and tasty, as well as looking beautiful when in flower. He pops the classic pink and white speckled beans into small pots of compost, on their ends, 1½ inches (4 cm) deep. These are placed in the greenhouse or on a sunny windowsill and watered. Kept moist, they should start to sprout in a few days. Dirty Nails won't consider planting them outside until after 12 May because they are very tender and easily killed by a late frost.

Root Veg

Parsnips, sown in mid-March, are just beginning to show their first pair of small, pale green leaves. It is a hard job spotting them amongst the seedling weeds at this

NATURAL HISTORY IN THE GARDEN
Cow Parsley

Cow parsley will be growing well this month. Its fern-like foliage bursts out from around the bases of trees, under hedges, throughout areas of rough ground. As April passes, look out for the frothy flowers that reach up beyond the green leaves and dance atop them like a white mist. Each big flat platter of flowers is made up of half a dozen or more smaller flower heads, and each one of these consists of tiny individual florets.

VEGETABLE SNIPPETS
CATCH CROPS

stage, but Dirty Nails always makes an effort to clear around the tiny 'snips when they first emerge. It's a painstaking job, but well worth making the effort before the parsnip bed turns into a mini-jungle.

Dirty Nails has thinned his salsify and scorzonera this week too. They were sown in the first week of April and have germinated quickly. Two seeds were sown at 6 inch (15 cm) intervals, and by now they look like strands of grass. The weakest one has been pulled from each sowing station, the lines hoed and watered.

Catch crop is the term used to describe a rapidly maturing crop that can be sown at the same time as another, longer term, main crop, with the seeds of both mixed together. The two grow cheek-by-jowl but being much faster of growth, the catch crop is harvested and eaten way in advance of the main crop. Having become established, the remaining developing plants then have plenty of room in which to thrive and plump up.

To this end, salsify and scorzonera seeds can be comfortably mixed with those of lettuces or radishes, which are ideal catch crops. They won't impede the root veggies, which will occupy the ground for many months, but will increase the yield and variety of foodstuffs which any one piece of ground can produce.

SWEDES

This is the perfect time of year for planting swedes. Dirty Nails has been sowing seeds of the Marian variety this week. He likes to start his swedes in between rows of winter Radar onions. These are pretty well grown by now and will be harvested in June. The thick green onion tops provide good protection for the germinating swedes, and a sowing in early May will have a month or so to sprout and be thinned before the seedlings are exposed to the elements, and pigeons. These birds love swede tops. Once the onions are gone, Dirty Nails stops them from damaging his crops by running string between supporting posts to create a cobweb effect. This is thin enough to allow him to get in and weed, but thick enough to foil a landing pigeon's outstretched wings.

He also ties takeaway cartons to sticks for the purpose of bird-scaring.

Having thoroughly weeded his onions Dirty Nails 'station sows' his swede seeds three at a time, ¾ of an inch (2 cm) deep and 6 inches (15 cm) apart. Kept moist and with plenty of warm sunshine, they should be ready for thinning to the strongest seedling in 20 days or so. Further thinning will

NATURAL HISTORY IN THE GARDEN
Stinging Nettle

After April showers come May flowers, and a vast array of common yet fascinating plants can transform the garden into a colourful wonderland this month. The stinging nettle grows abundantly in and around human habitation, and has done so for centuries. It thrives in the rich soils that are invariably created near where folk live. The stinger is covered with tiny hairs all over. Even the faintest of touches will break the tips of these hairs and release a potent acid which is both painful and can cause a rash. However it is an important food source for many beautiful species of butterfly when in their caterpillar form, and people have used nettles through the ages for cloth, food and medicine. The delicious young tips can be pinched out and eaten, the sting being rendered harmless through steaming.

be needed in a few weeks to allow 12 inches (30 cm) between plants.

Swedes grow vigorously. They will swell up, and with luck should provide a heavy yield of cream and purple-skinned, deep yellow-fleshed roots that are ready for harvesting from October onwards. Swedes are very hardy vegetables and can be left in the ground until needed in the kitchen.

VEGETABLE SNIPPETS
A BRIEF HISTORY OF
THE SWEDE

The swede (*Brassica napus*) is alternatively known to Americans as rutabaga and to the Scots as neeps. In northern England it is rather confusingly referred to as turnip.

Some sources locate the development of swedes to seventeenth century Bohemia, where it was described as a cross between a cabbage and a turnip. By 1664 this vegetable was being cultivated in Britain and was popular across the colder northern European countries where it does well. Relatively easy to grow and hardy, swedes were an important staple of the war-time diet between 1939 and 1945 and are rich in vitamin A. The young leaves also make a hearty meal when taken and treated as for cabbage.

A WORD FROM THE FLOWER GARDEN

May, 2nd Week

This week Mrs Nails has been tidying up the long sprawling remains of her daffodils. In their full splendour the various varieties have sung the song of spring, and made the walk to Dirty Nails' vegetable patch a true delight. However there is little more displeasing to her eye than that which is left behind, deflecting from the glory of the bluebells and shading shoots of irises yet to come into their own.

The challenge for Mrs Nails is to fold and gently tie without using any string or bruising the leaves. It is tempting to cut them away, especially of the larger varieties, but beware! Such a measure may provide instant neatness, but the bulb (and, subsequently, next season's produce) will not thank you for the lack of essential nutrients and goodness that it needs to reabsorb to thrive year after year.

Allowing time for the foliage to soften, Mrs Nails divides each group of stems and leaves and folds them either twice or thrice, using a couple of the softest outer leaves as ties to hold them in place. It is a skill that may take some practice, but be patient. Next spring your garden will repay you with a reward of golden delight.

NATURAL HISTORY IN THE GARDEN
White Dead-Nettle

The white dead-nettle looks similar to the stinger at first glance, but is actually quite different. It is a member of the mint family. This month it sports clusters of white, hooded, flask-like flowers up the stem. It is much sought after by bumble bees and has adapted its flowers especially for them. When the bee dips down into the depths of the flower for a sip of nectar, pollen is brushed onto the fluffy insect's back by stamens (the male part) which are concealed beneath the hood. As the bee works amongst other dead-nettles, it mixes pollen from different flowers onto the styles (female part) of others, so ensuring that pollination occurs.

VEGETABLE SNIPPETS
TALKING WEEDS

Weeds are described as ephemeral, annual or perennial.

Ephemeral weeds

Ephemeral weeds are very short-lived and sometimes called ruderals. These pioneering plants are among the first to colonise open soil. They can complete their life cycle in any month of the year, often producing several generations in one season. For example, chickweed can flower and set seed every five to six weeks, spawning on average 2,500 seeds per plant. Hairy bitter cress and groundsel are similarly short-lived and rapid reproducers, spilling an average of 600 and 1,500 seeds respectively every few weeks. All these ruderals are especially prolific in the months between April and October.

Annual weeds

Annual weeds cannot survive the cold of UK winters. They are adapted to grow, set seed and die over the course of one season. Wild flowers such as poppies, fat hen (Good King Henry) and cleavers (also known as sticky-buds, or goose grass) are examples of annuals. They over-winter as seeds which are produced in abundance.

Perennials

Perennials persist from year to year. Slower growing than the other types of weed, species such as dandelion and dock survive the winter cold and summer heat thanks to their thick, fleshy roots in which they gather and store reserves of nutrients and moisture. The daisy, so common and lovely in the lawn, is a perennial flower that stashes winter supplies in fibrous roots.

TURNIPS AND RUNNERS

May, 3rd Week

Turnips

This has been a very exciting week for Dirty Nails. Turnips of the F1 Market Express variety were sown in trays in the greenhouse around mid-February, and then planted outside a month later. The golf-ball sized roots, slightly conical and creamy coloured with a pinky-purple top, have all been pulled and eaten over the last few days. F1 Market Express is an extremely fast growing 'nip which can be ready for harvesting and eating 50 days or so after sowing.

Dirty Nails will be sowing turnips in short lines every couple of weeks until June. He rakes the seedbed into a fine tilth, and sows the round, brown seeds, each the size of a pinhead, thinly and direct into a ½ inch (2 cm) deep drill. 'Nips like plenty to drink so he keeps them well watered. When the seedlings have appeared, he thins them out to final spacings of 3 inches (8 cm) to give them room to swell. Pigeons are partial to turnip tops so he always protects them with twigs or wire netting.

Runner beans

Runner beans have been planted out this week too.

They have come on well in their pots and are showing two pairs of leaves. Dirty Nails is growing his runners against a south-west facing fence, up canes 8 inches (20 cm) apart. He prepared the ground early in the year by trench composting. This involved

NATURAL HISTORY IN THE GARDEN
Badgers in May

Badger cubs are now emerging from their setts with increasing confidence. As they explore this new world above ground, the young badgers will be closely watched by their parents, in much the same way as mums keep an eye on toddlers playing in the garden.

almost filling the dug-out growing area with kitchen and garden waste, and topping up with soil. He is hoping that this goodness in the ground will feed the hungry bean plants and give a bumper crop. They need some training until they get themselves wrapped around the canes, but there is little else to do now except keep moist, weed-free and wait with eager anticipation.

Having a fleece handy, ready to throw over the beans or hardening-off courgettes if there is a risk of a late frost, is a good idea and could save a tender crop.

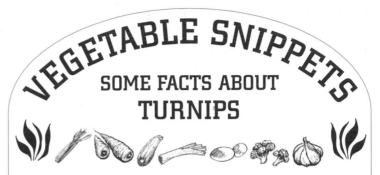

VEGETABLE SNIPPETS
SOME FACTS ABOUT
TURNIPS

Humans have cultivated turnips for thousands of years on account of the plump, edible, swollen stalk (not actually a root at all) which makes such good eating. They have been a feature of the European diet since Neolithic times, some 3000 BC. In the East wild turnips are recorded as being raised as a crop in India since 1500 BC. The seeds were pressed to produce cooking oil. Ancient Greeks and Romans enjoyed the culinary virtues of this plant too.

Turnips grow well in temperate climates across the world, and in northern Europe were a staple foodstuff of the poor until the 1500s when potatoes arrived from the Americas. In the 1800s what is now central London was a sea of veg. Turnips were intensively raised in the market gardens of the area at that time.

COURGETTES, NETTLES AND COMFREY

May, 4th Week

Courgettes

Dirty Nails has planted out his courgettes this week. They had been put outside for a few days beforehand with protection at night. The young plants were filling their 3 inch (8 cm) pots and showing three or four true leaves.

Dirty Nails plants his courgettes in holes 2 feet (60 cm) apart with a dollop of compost at the bottom. He carefully holds the pots with his fingers, supporting the stem at pot-rim level, and turns them upside-down. A couple of taps on the bottom releases the plant, and the root-balls can be popped easily into the holes. He firms the soil around each one, gently. These are thirsty plants and to make watering easier and less wasteful, Dirty Nails earths up a little ridge of soil to form a ring around each courgette plant. This stops water from running away and is especially helpful if the vegetables are grown on sloping ground.

Nettles and comfrey

Elsewhere on the plot Dirty Nails has an old wormery bin which he is regularly topping up with freshly cut stinging nettle and comfrey leaves. As these ferment within, the resulting juice they produce gathers at the bottom. This is a highly potent and traditional plant food. The tincture is strained off as and when needed. A cupful stirred into a 2 gallon watering can will be a real boost for those newly planted out courgettes. Dirty Nails gives all his veg regular nettle and comfrey feeds once they are past the tender seedling stage.

NATURAL HISTORY IN THE GARDEN
Leaves

Everywhere is turning different shades of green as buds burst out on trees, leaves unfold and stretch themselves. Each leaf is like an individual solar panel, absorbing sunlight energy and using it to convert carbon dioxide in the air and water into growth-enabling carbohydrates. This is a process called photosynthesis and the by-product is oxygen, which is essential to life itself.

VEGETABLE SNIPPETS

MORE ABOUT COMFREY

Bocking 14 is a sterile form of comfrey. As it does not go to seed, there is no risk of it spreading wildly and taking over the veg plot. However it regenerates easily from portions of root, so care must be exercised to avoid spreading fragments to places where they are not wanted (the compost heap, for example) when digging in the area of this plant.

Comfrey tincture is especially high in potassium (K). This important nutrient is an essential ingredient for veggies that flower, set seed, or fruit, such as tomatoes and courgettes. Farmyard manure (FYM) is an alternative source of K, but comfrey is a much richer source, two or three times so. One reason for this is that the extensive roots plunge down deep into the soil, and can access nutrient reserves which would otherwise be out of bounds. Dredged up thus, nutrients are transferred into the leaves and are then made available in the soil when the leaves decompose.

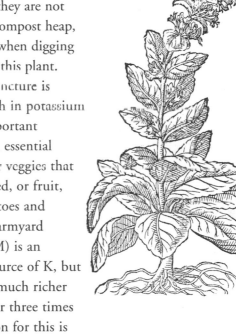

PURPLE SPROUTING BROCCOLI AND BROAD BEANS

Purple sprouting broccoli

Purple sprouting, steamed and served up in the spring or early summer with a knob of margarine melted over, is a food experience which Dirty Nails awaits eagerly each year. In order to enjoy this seasonal pleasure, he has been planting out his young purple sprouting specimens into their final growing positions this week. He raised them by popping the pinhead sized brown seeds into 3 inch (7½ cm) pots of compost in the greenhouse around mid-April, and keeping moist. It is a bit late to sow from seed now, but seedlings are often available at markets and plant sales.

Dirty Nails digs over his bed and weeds it thoroughly. Next he treads the soil down to a firm surface with small sideways footsteps back and forth. The young plants are then put into the soil with 2 feet (60 cm) between them. A hole is dug with a trowel, and the plants lowered down. He fills the hole with water at this stage and waits for it to be absorbed before carefully filling in with soil and firming. Dirty Nails plants his purple sprouting deep enough so that the seed leaves, if they have not already turned yellow and dropped off, are either buried or at soil level.

Cabbage root fly is a danger to the transplants at this stage. They like to lay their eggs around the base of any brassicas. The hatching maggots burrow down to the roots where they settle and feed. The plant is either killed or weakened to the point of being useless. In order to prevent this from happening Dirty Nails fits small collars around each plant base. He makes them from carpet underlay cut into 4 inch (10 cm) squares, with a long slit to slide in snugly but not too tightly. Pigeons are kept off with string stretched between

NATURAL HISTORY IN THE GARDEN
Cuckoo in the Nest

The female cuckoo will be busy from the end of May. She seeks out the nests of small birds and, when the coast is clear, will fly down to eject one of the eggs. This is replaced with one of her own which is incubated, hatched and raised by the unknowing host. Mrs Cuckoo might lay up to a dozen eggs in a dozen different nests.

May, 5th Week

sticks in a criss-cross fashion, and plastic bags tied onto canes. Dirty Nails will be keeping a close eye on his purple sprouting and, with all being well, he should be cutting the unopened flower heads in about nine months' time.

Broad beans

Broad beans which were planted in the first week of March are now flowering in profusion. Each flower is potentially a full pod of beans. Dirty Nails is giving his broads plenty of water at this flowering stage, which helps the crop to fatten up nicely.

VEGETABLE SNIPPETS

CABBAGE ROOT FLY

The cabbage root fly is called *Delia radicum*. Adults on the wing are rarely noticed, but their effects are a highly visible and upsetting feature in the cabbage patch every year, despite precautions. All members of the brassica family, including swedes, kale and Brussels sprouts, may be selected as fodder for their grubs. Affected plants fail to grow properly and have a listless, wilted appearance. At this point even a gentle tug will unearth a rotten stump where a mass of strong roots should be. The plant is fit only for burning. A peppering of white maggots on this stump, or in the immediately adjacent soil, reveals the culprits.

There may be three generations of this common garden pest wreaking havoc on the plot between spring and autumn. Females scout for suitable food plants, which may also include ornamentals such as wallflowers. Seedlings or fresh transplants are her preferred option. Once located, she lays her eggs on the soil surface around the stem. These hatch in due course, whereupon they burrow down and start munching. If left undisturbed, they will pupate (change into adults) underground and emerge to perpetuate the damage. Closely fitted collars of carpet underlay act as a physical barrier. The eggs are prevented from reaching the soil. They dry up and perish instead of hatching.

BLACKFLY ON BROAD BEANS

Blackfly can completely devastate a crop of broad beans at this time of year. They are the great enemy of broads. At flowering time masses of these irritating sap-sucking pests can descend on a crop and extract the life out of the beans as they form. It does not happen every year, but Dirty Nails has suffered such heartbreak, and tries a number of ways to avoid this problem.

In years when blackfly is rife, he pinches out the growing tips of his plants and burns them. This removes the most tender bit which the blackfly like best. For other affected areas, he makes up a weak washing-up liquid and water dilution and dispenses this with a hand-held mist sprayer. He does this on a daily basis, but it is not always satisfactory. The most successful tactic Dirty Nails has used to beat blackfly is to sow broad beans direct into the ground during November. This way a variety such as Aquadulce will grow on slowly throughout the winter months and produce pods for picking a fortnight or so earlier than a spring-sown crop. The important thing is that autumn-sown broads are usually productive before blackfly are a problem. If they do clash, the advanced state of growth renders these broads more able to withstand attack.

In some years Dirty Nails has had to write off his spring-sown Witkiem. All is not lost however, as elsewhere on the veg plot Aquadulce is already feeding the family and there is hardly a blackfly in sight.

NATURAL HISTORY IN THE GARDEN
Cuckoo spit

Dripping globs of frothy spittle appear on grasses and plant stems all over the garden in June. Known as cuckoo spit, it is actually the work of an insect called the common froghopper. These sap-sucking bugs are mottled in their adult form, but the cuckoo spit hides and protects their tiny green larvae. The mass of bubbly goo is exuded from the anus of the juvenile froghopper.

VEGETABLE SNIPPETS

THE FASCINATING
WORLD OF APHIDS

Aphids are true bugs, also known as blackfly. They are a major pest of both farmers' field and kitchen garden, but are also amazing creatures in their own right. They provide a major source of sustenance for useful species such as ladybirds, lacewings and hoverflies, which can be encouraged onto the veg patch with the allied provision of suitable flowering plants and habitat. Insect eating birds like blue tits may depend on them in hard times during winter, when they flock to the hedgerows and shrub borders, acrobatically eking out a meagre ration. Ants 'farm' them, protecting vast herds on the stems and underside of leaves. Using their antennae to stroke their charges, the ants receive a sugar-loaded drink of honeydew direct from the aphid's anus.

Honeydew is the sap which constantly flows around a plant. It is accessed by the aphid via its needle-like mouthpart, a hollow tube that is thrust into the tender host. Viruses are often transmitted from plant to plant by dirty 'needles'. Honeydew is rich in sugar and low in protein. In order to achieve satisfaction, enormous amounts must be consumed. Happily for the insects, it circulates at such a rapid rate that it is constantly dripping out of the feeding hordes. This is why plant foliage is often sticky in the summer, especially on trees like sycamore, and can be the cause of mouldy fungal growth later on. Weakened by these mass gatherings, infested plants often appear weakened, twisted and gnarled.

In mild winters aphids may pass the coldest months as adults feeding amongst plot-side weeds. More usually, however, they over-winter as eggs. Spindle is a favourite host plant, but ornamental lilacs and *Vibernum* species are also popular. In spring aphid nymphs are born as already-pregnant females. This is called parthenogenesis (virgin birth). A fortnight or so later, winged youngsters are being brought forth too. These take to the air and find other host plants for a summer of feasting.

Aphids can be found in profusion on spinach, wild flowers such as thistles, poppies, dock, cultivated domestic roses and many other herbaceous plants. As the season turns towards autumn the bugs respond to decreasing daylight hours and temperatures by bearing winged males and females. They fly off, mate, and deposit eggs on a suitable host, whereby the cycle of life, death and rebirth continues for another year.

PLANTING OUT LEEKS

June, 2nd Week

Dirty Nails has been planting out his first batch of leeks into the main bed this week. He grows a number of varieties to crop from September through to March. The tall, strong, long-shafted Axima will be harvestable well before New Year, and then the thicker, heavier Giant Winter variety will supply the kitchen until the spring. Carentan 2 is an autumn cropping leek which Dirty Nails grows in order to eat as baby leeks in July. The Mammoth variety can grow to be the size of a person's arm and will take some eating. He is cultivating a few of these as a novelty.

Dirty Nails sowed the small black seeds in trays indoors from February to early April, and then transplanted them into a nursery bed when they were like blades of grass. With those Axima leeks now the size of pencils, this is the right time to get them into their final growing positions. Dirty Nails dug over the bed, weeded it thoroughly, sprinkled wood ash over it and raked to a fine tilth. He plants these early leeks at 6 inch (15 cm) intervals in rows set a foot (30 cm) apart. A broken spade handle with a rounded-off end is used to push into the soil to a depth of 6 inches (15 cm). The seedling leeks are popped into these, one to a hole.

Dirty Nails then puddles them in, which involves filling each hole

NATURAL HISTORY IN THE GARDEN
Badgers in June

This is a month of plenty for badgers. Although classified as carnivores, badgers will in fact eat almost anything and they have a sweet tooth (they are omnivores). Household scraps and kitchen waste are popular around human dwellings, as well as beetles, grubs, roots, bulbs and sweet veggies such as carrots. Young rabbits and moles will be dug out and dined upon, if available, and fruit becomes a major portion of their diet later in the year. Wasp and bee nests built into the ground are much sought after. But a badger's food of choice is the humble earthworm, which is sucked up like a string of spaghetti.

VEGETABLE SNIPPETS

NURSERY BEDS

with water. As this soaks in the roots will settle down. Careful puddling-in daily for a week or so will be worth the effort because leeks respond well to generous watering at this stage. His other varieties will be planted out similarly in a fortnight or so at 8 inch (20 cm) intervals, except Carentan 2 which will go directly from the nursery bed into the kitchen.

All that leeks require from now on is to be kept moist and weed-free.

Nursery beds bridge the gap between seedling and developing young adult. They are areas of the veg patch set aside for nursing seedlings through from pricking out from trays to planting out in the main plot. Hardy crops like leeks and brassicas (the 'cabbage tribe') are classic benefactors from this system of husbandry, where small plants can be lovingly nurtured through their most tender stages under a close and watchful eye.

A high density of veggies can be cultivated in this small area, with careful attention paid to weed control and watering. In many respects this process is like potting-on into a larger container (which is a method Dirty Nails uses to bring on his courgettes and squashes before nestling them into the ground as soon as the risk of frost has passed).

Handling at all times must be done with a deft touch. Seedlings are especially vulnerable to damage and bruising. Light manoeuvring, only holding the leaves, is essential, and roots should be kept as intact as possible. By the time they are ready to move on they should be tough little customers. Nonetheless a considered fork must be skilfully employed to loosen and lift the roots. With leeks, Dirty Nails gathers them up in bunches and wraps his charges in damp newspaper to bridge the gap between nursery and main bed.

KOHLRABI

This week Dirty Nails has been sowing kohlrabi. This unusual looking vegetable is a member of the cabbage family and is also known as turnip-rooted cabbage. It is a quick growing green veg which has a swollen stem base with leaves growing from bracts around the middle and a tuft on top. The leaves are discarded in the kitchen and the bulbous part eaten. It is delicious steamed, sautéd or eaten raw either grated or cut into thin slices.

Dirty Nails grows the Delikatess variety, and sows seeds thinly in a shallow drill ½ inch (1½ cm) deep. Shallow sowing is important, to allow the stem bases room to swell. When he sows more than one row, he spaces them a foot (30 cm) apart. As the seedlings grow and develop true leaves, Dirty Nails thins them to allow 6 inches (15 cm) between plants. Larger spacings can produce bigger crops, but kohlrabi is at its best when the bulbs are not much bigger than a golf ball. It copes with dry conditions better than most veg although Dirty Nails spares them whatever water he can because this makes them all the more tender.

He is now pulling kohlrabi sown in March and looking forward to a late summer harvest from this week's sowing. A further line or two sown at the end of July should supply the kitchen into winter, and kohlrabi is hardy enough to stand in the ground until needed.

NATURAL HISTORY IN THE GARDEN
Wolf Spider

A compact spider which is commonly found scurrying around on bare earth or amongst low-growing plants such as speedwell is the wolf spider. This spider does not make a web. Instead, it catches its prey by running it into submission. Female wolf spiders carry their eggs around in a silken ball held close to their bodies and are easily recognisable by this habit. Several species of wolf spider even allow the young spiderlings to hitch a lift on their backs for a week or more after hatching.

VEGETABLE SNIPPETS
SOME FACTS ABOUT
KOHLRABI

This unusual looking brassica takes its name from the German *kohl*, meaning cabbage, and *rabi*, which means turnip. Scientifically known as *Brassica oleracea va. caulo-rapa*, it was developed by selective breeding as a food crop in northern Europe during the fifteenth and sixteenth centuries. By the late 1700s, kohlrabi was being cultivated in Britain. Although not commonly consumed on these shores it is popular fare today in continental Europe.

POTTERING, TENDING RUNNER BEANS, JERUSALEM ARTICHOKES AND COURGETTES

Dirty Nails is enjoying having time to potter around. There is a definite lull in the vegetable garden now that the rush of spring planting is over, and crops are harvestable all over the place. By sowing seeds of different crops a little and often, Dirty Nails has his lettuces, turnips, radishes, beetroot, kohlrabi and others at different stages of growth from seedling onwards. This succession-sowing avoids a wasteful glut and ensures that there is fresh veg in the ground ripening over the whole summer.

Runner beans

The runner beans have grown to the top of their supporting canes. This is the time to pinch the growing tip out, to concentrate the bean's energy into flower production. Even if it has rained a lot they benefit from a good daily watering. Once in flower, add a splosh of nettle-and-comfrey concentrate to the watering can every couple or three days.

Jerusalem artichokes

Dirty Nails has cut about 1½ feet (45 cm) off the top of his Jerusalem artichokes. These have grown thick, tall, leafy tops since being planted early in the year. They are quite susceptible to wind damage during summer storms so reducing their height now will lessen the risk of snapping.

Courgettes

Dirty Nails' courgettes are beginning to fruit and he has put a straw mulch

NATURAL HISTORY IN THE GARDEN
House martins

House martins

Similar to swifts, but smaller and more fluttery in flight, are house martins. Viewed from the ground they appear black and white in colour, with shorter wings and a distinctive V-tail. House martins fly fast too, wheeling and twisting, arching and curling in the air. They trawl the skies for food with their mouths wide open, resembling penguins diving for fish in another element.

These birds make their nests close to people, in an enclosed cup-shaped nest tucked under house eaves. Martins are top-notch builders and they construct their breeding chamber out of stuck-together balls of mud. However too much

June, 4th Week

around the plants. This has the dual purpose of conserving moisture, which courgettes suck up with great gusto, as well as keeping the rapidly forming and prolific fruits clean off the soil. The risk of blossom-end rot and slug damage is thus reduced.

Any hot dry spell now sees Dirty Nails busy with his hoe. Fewer weeds means more space and goodness for the veg!

tidiness in the countryside and a dry spell in late spring can be disastrous for them because they need to locate mud of just the right texture from pond margins and dirty farmyards.

VEGETABLE SNIPPETS
MORE ABOUT WEEDS

A weed can be defined as a plant of any kind which is growing in the wrong place. There are many examples of this situation including chickweed smothering lettuces, moss in the lawn and last year's spuds in amongst current crops such as leaf beet. All weeds compete with cultivated plants for the three essential requirements of life: water, nutrients, light.

Some have what is called 'allelopathic' (poisonous) tendencies. The roots of such species produce chemicals that inhibit either the germination, growth or development of their neighbours. This can include veggies. Allelopathic plants include creeping buttercup, couch grass (sometimes called twitch), creeping thistle and chickweed. Rhododendron is the classic poisonous plant. Introduced as cover for pheasants, it takes over large areas if left unchecked and is of poor wildlife value.

Pests and diseases can often be harboured on weeds. Fungal rust, an orangey powder that coats leaves, can affect garlic and leeks. It also thrives on groundsel, for instance. Fat hen (also known as Good King Henry) and dock frequently host vast armies of aphids which then home in on runner and broad bean crops.

CABBAGE WHITE BUTTERFLIES

July, 1st Week

Dirty Nails has some fine, healthy young specimens of purple sprouting broccoli. They were planted out at the end of May and now stand around a foot (30 cm) in height with thick stems and juicy, broad leaves. The pigeons have been deterred by lines of string criss-crossing over them between sticks and, dangling on canes, takeaway cartons that move and make a noise in the breeze. Rabbits are having an occasional nibble, but mercifully not doing any serious damage yet.

The big thing that Dirty Nails looks out for on all his brassicas from now onwards is butterfly damage. Two butterflies lay their eggs on purple sprouting and other members of the cabbage tribe: the large and small white. They are on the wing now, sniffing out their favourite food-plants.

The large white lays its tiny yellow eggs in clusters that are easy to detect on the underside of leaves. When the caterpillars hatch they eat their egg-cases and then start tucking into the leaf. At this stage they tend to feed together. As they grow they quickly spread out over the whole plant and can devastate it to the point of being a skeleton. The caterpillars are yellow and black.

The small white lays its minute eggs singly on the underside of the leaf. Its caterpillar is small and green. It takes some looking for. They are a particular problem on cabbages because they start feeding at the heart and then eat their way outwards.

Dirty Nails makes time at least twice a week to have a

NATURAL HISTORY IN THE GARDEN
Blackbirds

Keep an eye out for blackbirds congregating on the lawn this month, in groups of half a dozen or more. Members of the thrush family, the handsome males are glossy black with bright orange-yellow beaks and eye rings. Females are a duller brown.

Blackbirds like to hop, skip and jump over the turf, watching and listening for invertebrate movement. They will stand still and cock their heads, keeping a keen ear out for the faint rustle of earthworm activity, before pouncing and stabbing the ground, then tugging out a tasty morsel. A blackbird whose beak is dripping full with worms may well be feeding a newly fledged youngster nearby.

thorough hands-on check of his brassicas. He gently rubs out patches of eggs with his thumb, but will not squash the caterpillars once they have hatched. Instead, he uses a fine paintbrush to remove them into a jar and relocates them elsewhere in the garden, onto nasturtiums which they also love. He grows nasturtiums specifically for this job. This is a time-consuming task but it gives Dirty Nails real pleasure to be outside looking for caterpillars and listening to birdsong on a peaceful summer evening.

VEGETABLE SNIPPETS

LARGE WHITE LIFE CYCLE

Clouds of white butterflies mixing together above the cabbage patch, rising and falling in delicate dance, like bubbles of fizz in a glass of lemonade, used to be a far more common sight in our towns and gardens before the widespread use of insecticides put paid to vast numbers of these infuriating but beautiful insects. In the vicinity of suitable food-plants where chemicals are shunned or not used at all, the wildlife-friendly grower may be treated to the spectacle of a gathered knot or three of these charming customers, bobbing and weaving as they pass across his little piece of heaven, doing what they've always done, lending a delicious 'scene from yesteryear' taste to the garden landscape.

They are amazing creatures, make no mistake. Large whites develop from egg to adult, experiencing a change known as 'complete metamorphosis'. On the wing in April and May, having survived the winter as a chrysalis tucked away somewhere sheltered and safe, they mate. She lays batches of yellow eggs on the underside of brassica leaves, and in two weeks a mass of tiny caterpillars emerge with only one thing on their minds - to eat! This they do, non-stop, through June, growing quite large and distinctive.

When ready, the satiated caterpillars sneak away to hole-up in a handy crevice or woody cabbage stalk, to pupate. Forming a chrysalis to protect themselves during this most incredible transformation, they completely rearrange their bodies both inside and out, and emerge in July as the familiar cabbage white to wreak more havoc on the veg plot. A second generation of youngsters may prove more damaging than the first, and this lot generally over-winter in a chrysalis to commence the process again when early-summer next comes around.

Natural predators of the large white include starlings, which scoff lots of these pests as caterpillars, and wasps which snatch them as food for their grubs. Spiders also do a fine job of snaring the adults, paralysing them, and then sucking their bodily juices dry.

BULL-NECKED ONIONS AND THE LAST GLOBE ARTICHOKES

Bull-necked onions

Dirty Nails is pleased with the progress of his onions. He planted sets of Sturon, Stuttgarter Giant and Red Baron throughout March, and has kept the rows moist and weed-free since then. He popped the acorn-sized onion sets in at 6 inch (15 cm) intervals and they have thrived in this space. The bulbs are now mostly 3 to 4 inches (7 to 10 cm) across, with the odd few over 5 inches (12 cm). Whenever an onion has bolted and pushed up a flower head, Dirty Nails has pinched it off.

These bolting onions are a nuisance because they become 'bull-necked' and won't be any good for storing over the winter.

The bulbs develop a solid central core and thick, stiff, central stem. Dirty Nails finds that his Red Barons are more likely to bolt than the white varieties. Any bull-neckers can be left in the ground with the rest of the crop, but because they won't keep, they are worth pulling now as and when required for cooking, or to liven up summer salads.

NATURAL HISTORY IN THE GARDEN
Orange Hawkweed

Catching the eye with a vibrant display of cheery flowers in the banks around about is the orange hawkweed. This lovely little low grower displays vividly every year and should be on show this month. Another name for it is fox-and-cubs on account of the foxy coloured blooms and the way they form grouped bunches on their stalks.

July, 2nd Week

Globe artichokes
There are a couple of meal-sized flower buds remaining on the globe artichokes which have produced a good crop after an earlier than usual start. Dirty Nails will cut these within the next few days and enjoy the exquisite experience that eating these glorious, immature flower heads provides. After that, any other small buds will be removed to concentrate all the plant's energy back into itself, in readiness for hopefully another fine crop for next June and July.

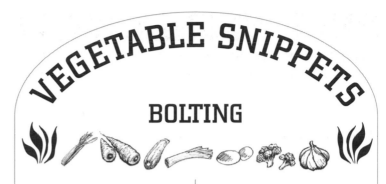

Vegetable Snippets

BOLTING

Bolting is a phenomenon which occurs in biennial plants. These are plants that grow for a season, rest (go dormant) for the winter, resume growth in the spring, then flower and set seed in the second summer. This includes onions, leeks and garlic, as well as many brassicas. Left to their own devices veggies like these will exhibit such behaviour.

Under normal circumstances the hungry gardener gets in there first, and harvests the crops while still young and tender. However where the environment is harsh, due to weather extremes such as drought or frost, biennials can become stressed and produce flowers in their first year. This is bolting, and it is a survival mechanism which has evolved as a way of securing the future of the species.

PERPETUAL SPINACH (LEAF BEET)

Perpetual spinach also goes under the name of leaf beet, which reflects the fact that it is not a member of the spinach family at all. It is closely related to beetroot, but the leaves are very similar to spinach in taste. Dirty Nails grows leaf beet instead of spinach as he finds it an easier and more reliable performer in the veg garden. It produces lovely big green leaves in profusion, and is far less prone to bolting during hot, dry spells. Dirty Nails sows leaf beet in March for cropping throughout the summer and this week has sown another couple of 6 foot (1.8 metre) rows. He will protect these later sowings throughout the winter under cloches and they should provide useful greens until the spring.

Leaf beet seeds are small and knobbly, but large enough to handle individually. Dirty Nails sows his in a sunny bed, in soil that has been raked to a fine tilth. The seeds are sown thinly in drills, not more than ½ an inch (1½ cm) deep, and kept well watered. He allows a foot (30 cm) between rows. As the seedlings develop he will thin them out to 8 inch (20 cm) spacings.

Care needs to be taken when the leaves are ready for eating. Dirty Nails likes to cut them off as low down as possible with a sharp knife to avoid disturbing the roots, which can happen with heavy-handed snapping and

NATURAL HISTORY IN THE GARDEN
Yarrow

Yarrow is a plant which flowers this month. It can be seen in gardens or just beyond as an escapee, blooming in patches. It bears dense platters of white-petalled flowers with pale yellow centres. These are borne on stems rising out of thick, soft, slightly grey-green fern-like foliage. It is a deeply rooted, drought resistant member of the daisy family.

Anglo-Saxons referred to yarrow as woundwort, believing that a compress of yarrow and grease would heal puncture wounds and cuts. It was also picked and brought indoors to drive away evil and sickness. In olden times yarrow was thought to protect one's heart from being broken by a lover.

July, 3rd Week

VEGETABLE SNIPPETS
SOME FACTS ABOUT
LEAF BEET

tugging. Another plus for leaf beet is in the kitchen. Because the leaves grow upright from the ground and are not deeply ridged, they tend to be a lot less gritty than spinach. They are delicious steamed with or without the stalks, which take slightly longer to become tender.

Perpetual spinach is a selectively bred descendant of the wild plant, sea beet, which is a coastal species. Sprawling and hairless, it blooms from summer to early autumn. The display is modest, with numerous small green and yellow flowers adorning a spike which issues forth centrally from a bunch of thick, fleshy, spatula-shaped, red-tinged, glossy leaves.

Cultivation and refining of the wild forerunner began way back in the Middle East some 2,000 years ago. Perpetual spinach is a member of the goosefoot family of plants, and these have an important role in human food production worldwide. Other goosefoots include Swiss chard, mangel-wurzels and a range of fleshy-rooted beets.

Each seed may give rise to a cluster of seedlings because leaf beet is 'multi-germ'. This means that contained within one seed is the potential to form many individuals. In the best interests of growing your own greens it is wise to let them all pop up and have a good look at them whilst they are still tiny. The strongest, most handsome specimen can then be selected at this stage as the plant to nurture, and lavish with care and attention. All the others can be carefully pinched or pulled out, with minimum disturbance to the roots of the one that will eventually be eaten.

LOTS OF BADGERS, BEETROOT, RUNNERS AND COURGETTES

Badgers

Badgers have been causing Dirty Nails problems of late. With their naturally sweet tooth, they have taken a shine to his young parsnips. These loveable rogues have been digging neat holes and turfing out the 4 to 5 inch (10 to13 cm) 'snips, nibbling them and then leaving them on the surface. A few 'snips have been dragged to the edge of the plot and eaten, with just the green tops discarded. It is upsetting to see lovingly tended crops vandalised like this.

However it is an annual problem and one that won't go away. Badgers are persistent creatures of habit, enjoying carrots, sweet corn and all manner of soft fruit.

As soon as they begin to lay into his crops, which is frequently anytime around midsummer, Dirty Nails takes what he calls badger precautions. This involves sinking jam jars into the soil amongst the veg and half-filling them with his own urine which he collects in a bucket. Most evenings, for the next couple of months,

Dirty Nails also takes an evening stroll around his veggies applying urine with a garden mist sprayer. Badgers are very shy of humans and the stinking liquid is an effective deterrent which is both free and limitless in supply.

Runner beans

Runner beans are beginning to produce pods in abundance now. Dirty Nails picks them daily before they become hard and stringy. This keeps his runners in maximum cropping condition with lots of flowers

NATURAL HISTORY IN THE GARDEN
SWIFTS

As July presses relentlessly on, and with the school holidays upon us, a heatwave can inspire flocks of swifts to gather in the skies above the garden. As well as feeding on a wealth of insect life, young birds will be testing their wings and strengthening their lungs in preparation for a long migration back to over-wintering quarters in the southern hemisphere. They are a joy to watch on hot days, screaming and swooping, climbing and diving, like a shape-shifting shoal of sickle-shaped fish in the deep blue sky of an English summer.

July, 4th Week

and developing beans.

Courgettes

Courgettes are fruiting pro-lifically too. As with runners, the more you pick, the more they produce. Yellow Gold Rush and deep-green Black Beauty are very much on the menu at this time of year. Dirty Nails likes to slice them thinly and flash-fry in olive oil, seasoning with black pepper and a splash of soy sauce for a delicious snack at any time of the day.

Beetroot

Beetroot are cropping thick and fast with plentiful supplies from now until autumn thanks to consistent succession sowing. In the kitchen Mrs Nails twists the leaves off about an inch (2½ cm) up the stalk. This prevents all the lovely beetroot-red juice from bleeding away whilst simmering to tenderness in the pot.

VEGETABLE SNIPPETS
BEETROOT RED

The vibrant beetroot-red stain that is so characteristic of this vegetable is a purple pigment which exists within the plants cells. Cutting through the root with a sharp knife breaks the cells. The pigment floods out and they are said to be bleeding. This can occur inside the human body as well as on the chopping board, staining both solid and liquid waste as it passes through. It is perfectly normal and harmless although the visual effects can be alarming! It is not unheard of for paramedics to get an emergency call from worried patients who are experiencing nothing more serious than the colourful conse-quences of indulging in the consumption of this swollen root veg.

Nutritionally, beetroot is rich in dietary fibre, vitamin C and a number of minerals. The leaves, when steamed as for spinach, provide an excellent source of iron and calcium.

ONIONS, SPRING ONIONS AND JERUSALEM ARTICHOKES

Onions

Onions are very much on Dirty Nails' mind at the moment. His main crops, Stuttgarter Giant, Sturon and Red Baron, are fat and shiny in the ground. Their tops are turning brown and withering and the bulbs are ripening beautifully in the hot sun. Dirty Nails lets his onion tops die back naturally with the crop still in the ground. When he planted them as sets in March they were popped in at 6 inch (15 cm) intervals, with a foot (30 cm) between rows. This generous spacing

has been paying dividends ever since, giving the plants ample room to grow and now letting in plenty of sunshine. Bending over the tops carefully at the neck, if soft enough, is another way to expose the crop to the sun.

Harvesting will take place soon, with a watchful eye on the weather. If the forecast suggests it is set fine for some time at the end of August, they will be happy left in the ground. If wet weather threatens the latter half of the month, Dirty Nails will opt to lift his

onions and hang them in a sheltered but airy place, in bunches, to dry.

Spring onions

Spring onions can still be sown. Dirty Nails likes to get in a quick-growing variety such as Guardsman, which can be pulled for autumn salads in October, or over-wintered with protection for a very early spring crop. He sows the pinhead-sized black seeds carefully, evenly and not too thickly, less than ½ an inch (1 cm) deep with 4 inches (10 cm) between rows. He

NATURAL HISTORY IN THE GARDEN
Wood Pigeons

Look out for wood pigeons. These handsome, fat, grey and pink birds like to sit in large trees on a hot summer afternoon or evening, wheezily and endlessly repeating their 'coo-coo-coo-cu-coo' song. Every now and then a woodie, with a clap of wings, will launch

itself into the air from the leafy canopy, swoop down, then fly up in an arc with wings outstretched. This up/flap, down/glide, undulating flight is typically circular and the pigeon returns from whence it came to continue its lazy calling.

August, 1st Week

finds that emptying the seeds into the palm of one hand and sowing with thumb and forefinger of the other is the easiest way.

At this time of year it is important to keep the germinating seeds moist. Grass-like shoots should appear within a few days.

Jerusalem artichokes

Jerusalem artichokes have put on so much growth that Dirty Nails has cut back the rampant top-growth again, by nearly a third. He does this because the thick, bushy stems are prone to being rocked about in strong summer winds. Knocking the height down a bit lessens the chances of serious wind damage.

VEGETABLE SNIPPETS
WILD ONIONS

The wild onion (*Allium vineale*) is alternatively known as crow garlic. It is a persistent weed of English and Welsh grasslands. This plant is a tough little customer, identifiable by papery-sheathed flower heads which rise out of grass-like tufts of green leaves. Within this wrap, or spathe, are contained small, pale pink flowers and a cluster of rice-grain sized, pointy-ended bulbs. Each of these has the potential to break free, fall to earth and develop independently.

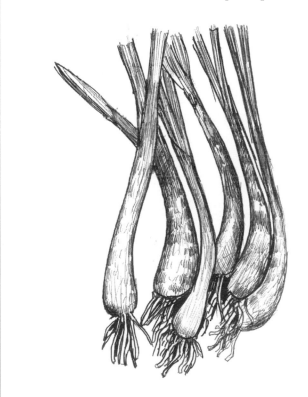

MOLES, MOLEHILLS AND WEEDING

August, 2nd Week

Moles and molehills

The moles which Dirty Nails has living in and around his veg patch are very busy at this time of year. Although their tunnelling can interfere with his root crops, he generally welcomes them. The soil which they push up into little mounds is of the finest quality: fresh, crumbly and virtually weed-free. Dirty Nails collects this molehill soil by shovelling it into old compost bags and storing these in an out-of-the-way, shaded corner. Molehills are very useful for bulking up potting compost and will be used in the spring for this purpose. Mixed with leaf-mould, they make a fine medium for growing on seedlings.

Moles do far more good than bad in the veg patch. They eat a lot of soil pests and their underground tunnels can assist with drainage in heavy soils. Moles can coexist with surface-rooting crops such as beans and greens quite happily. However if moles do move into part of the veg patch where they are not welcome, such as a parsnip or asparagus bed, Dirty Nails moves them on. To do this, he pushes freshly cut elder sticks and twigs into the molehills, and also any tunnels if they are visible close to the surface. This simple method has proved effective time and time again although he cannot explain why.

NATURAL HISTORY IN THE GARDEN
Wasps

Wasps have been spending most of the spring and early summer nest building and hunting out caterpillars and grubs to feed their larvae. In return, the larvae produce a sweet honeydew for the workers to feed on. However at this time of year the queen winds down her egg laying, and so the wasps need to seek out alternative sources of sweet food. They are far more visible now as sugary drinks and snacks, taken into the garden to enjoy in the open air, become an alternative form of sustenance for them.

When being hassled by scavenging wasps, it is worth remembering that each colony of up to 2,000 individuals accounts for many thousands of insect pests every year.

VEGETABLE SNIPPETS
FARMYARD MANURE (FYM)

Weeding

The hoe is being kept busy annihilating weeds during dry spells. A useful tool for delicate hoeing in tight spaces is a dinner knife, with the blade bent at 90 degrees halfway along its length. Dirty Nails uses his to slice the weeds off just below the soil surface with a controlled scraping motion. He uses a hoe to weed between rows, and a bent knife to get in between the individual plants.

When the soil is moist, most weeds will pull out whole with a bit of gentle persuasion. If the root is particularly deep Dirty Nails employs a hand-fork to loosen the soil just enough to tease the root out. He keeps an old dinner-fork in his pocket too, to use for exactly the same purpose, when soil disturbance needs to be kept to a minimum.

Farmyard manure (FYM) is quite possibly the best organic matter which vegetable growers can lay their hands on. In the olden times, when horsepower was the order of the day, it was widely and readily available. In 1950 as mechanisation kicked in after the Second World War, there were still 300,000 horses working on farms, according to government statistics. Nowadays a working horse is a novelty. FYM can be difficult to get hold of, but is well worth tracking down.

FYM has many virtues apart from being a slow-release fertiliser that contains all the essential nutrients demanded for healthy veg growth. The bulky nature of the stuff aids soil moisture retention. Healthy soil literally teems with life, and good old fashioned 'muck' is a dynamic improver of soil organism populations. FYM maintains and boosts the structure too, assisting with both breaking up heavy growing mediums and binding those which are light.

However a little care is a necessary precaution. Nutrient values can vary from load to load depending on the proportions of faeces, urine, straw and other bedding contained therein. FYM must also be well decomposed or else it can release ammonia and other toxic substances which are by-products given off by the army of microscopic creatures which are actively breaking it down. Lastly, FYM is dirty and heavy to handle so watch your back when loading and unloading.

STORING ONIONS AND SOWING GREEN MANURE

Storing onions

Dirty Nails is relieved that he made time to harvest his onions before the fine weather broke around the middle of this month. Onions are ripe for harvesting when the shiny bulbs with browned-off tops lift easily from the ground, and the roots are withered and dry. He sorts his onions out before tying them in bunches and hanging them in a sheltered and airy place to dry completely. A few always come up soft and mushy and these go straight onto the compost heap. Others may be soft and brownish under the papery skin around the neck and are liable to suffer neck rot in store. These are put aside for consumption first, as are any that have bolted and have a thick, stiff central stem.

The vast majority are usually fine however, and will be ready to store for the winter in a frost-free shed, suspended from the beams. If he has more onions than can be comfortably hung, Dirty Nails will keep them one-deep in fruit trays. Stored this way after a good season, onions should last well into early next summer.

Green manure

With a large area of the veg garden now empty, a green manure crop can be sown. This is not grown for eating, but to replenish or improve the soil. Green manures are usually hoed off and/or dug into the plot before they flower.

NATURAL HISTORY IN THE GARDEN
Slow Worms

Slow worms are resident dwellers in and around the wilder, rougher parts of Dirty Nails' veg plot. They may be chanced upon as they bask on the sun-kissed banks this month. In spite of their snake-like appearance slow worms are in fact legless lizards and totally harmless to humans.

A large specimen may be finger-thick and nearly a foot (30 cm) in length. The skin is fairly uniform in colour, ranging from brown-gold through to silver-grey, and although made up of tiny scales it is silky smooth to the touch. If startled, slow worms will glide effortlessly into the thick sward. From the moment they are born their favourite food is slugs which are consumed in vast quantities.

August, 3rd Week

Dirty Nails likes to scatter seeds of *Phacelia* onto open ground at this time of year. It is a quick growing plant that will suppress weeds and can be dug in during the autumn or left to over-winter. He likes *Phacelia* especially because inevitably some will be allowed to bloom. The delicate blue flowers start off like a tufted bud and then unfurl into a long tongue of tiny flowers which beneficial insects adore.

VEGETABLE SNIPPETS
MORE FACT ABOUT ONIONS

Gasses released by broken cells in the preparation of onions in the kitchen are the causes of crying at this time. Dirty Nails finds that chewing on a hunk of bread, without swallowing, calms the stinging irritation. He employs this tactic when onions are on the chopping board and it works every time although he is not sure exactly how or why.

The potent and flavoursome layers which make up an onion are actually modified leaves in which the plant stores supplies of food and water to survive the winter. The stem of an onion is internal. It is that bit just above the roots from which the edible leaves arise.

In the agricultural depression from 1348 to 1500, caused when the black death wiped out nearly half of the entire UK population, onions were an important ingredient in stews cooked up by the poor folk of those Medieval times. Known as pottage, it included whatever veg could be grown in a small piece of land set aside for growing food, called a pottager. According to the season, pottage typically consisted of onions, garlic, colewort, leeks, parley, scallions, carrot, parsnip, turnip, chervil, chives and rosemary.

FLOWERS IN THE VEG PATCH

August, 4th Week

Dirty Nails loves traditional agricultural weeds like poppies, corn cockle, cornflower, corn marigold and the wild pansy, heartsease. These

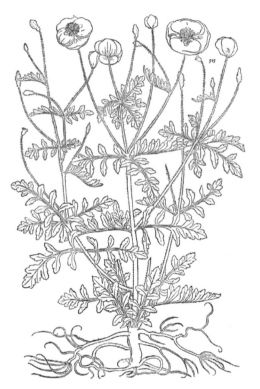

flowers grew in vast numbers before the use of weedkillers became widespread. If given a chance they will still thrive on regularly disturbed land and are very at home growing in amongst his vegetables. Dirty Nails does not allow these flowers to take over, and is constantly weeding them out. However he always allows a few specimens of his favourite species to bloom and set seed.

This week he has been collecting the ripe seeds of corn cockle and heartsease so he can sow them and grow them where he wants to next year. He gathers

NATURAL HISTORY IN THE GARDEN
Badgers in August

At about 6 kg (13.2 lb) badger cubs will have reached about half their adult weight by the beginning of this month. Badgers are often seen at night as they patrol the gardens and neighbourhood. Dry weather causes foraging further afield, while back at home they will be busy extending and renovating their setts.

flower seeds during dry sunny weather, shaking them into paper bags. Wild flowers in the veg patch can be very pleasing to look at and will attract all sorts of bees and other useful insects. He is convinced that growing wild flowers and veg together like this creates a healthy, naturally balanced environment.

The calendula, or pot marigold, which Dirty Nails grows around the edges of his veg patch, are now thick with both flowers and ripe seeds. This plant is grown to stop encroaching couch grass, which cannot tolerate residing in amongst calendula roots. He has been filling jam jars with their dry seeds, in preparation for sowing next spring. This will not only keep the plot free of troublesome couch, but also saves Dirty Nails a packet on purchasing seeds.

VEGETABLE SNIPPETS
RED MASON BEE (OSMIA RUFA)

The red mason bee, *Osmia rufa*, is a highly beneficial and hard-working insect which is worth commandeering into action amongst the veggies. Crops that depend on flowering to produce a cache of nutritious food will be serviced by these fellows, from peas and beans through to all manner of lovely fruits.

Purpose-built nests are available from specialist firms and good garden centres. They consist of a plastic cylinder which contains cardboard straws, typically 30 or 100, and it is these that provide a potential nursery for the young bees. Such contraptions imitate naturally occurring nesting sites which in the wild include hollow plant stems and beetle holes in wood.

Red mason bees are commonly seen in the vicinity of old walls and outbuildings. They can be observed passing in and out of little holes in the masonry. However, contrary to popular belief, they are not responsible for excavating these cavities themselves. The mining work is largely done by the solitary, white-banded Davies' colletes, one of eight UK species of *colletes* bee.

The red masons simply clean out and renovate suitable sites in the crumbly mortar of old brick and stonework, where they lay their eggs in self-sufficient chambers which they construct (empty nail or vine-eye holes are other favourites).

Proprietary nests secured to a south- or west-facing fence or shed at or above chest height in early spring are sure to attract mason and also leaf-cutter bees.

Red masons are busy in low temperatures when bumble bees hunker down and remain inactive. Their peak period for useful toil, as far as the home-producer is concerned, coincides with a wide range of top-fruit blossom (apples, pears, plums and the like), and one red mason is reputed to do the pollination work of 140 honey-bee workers. With no sting (they don't produce honey so have no need to defend their stores) they are safe and harmless around children and family areas in the garden.

ROOT VEG

Now is a good time to have a thorough weeding and tidying session in amongst the root veg, which is what Dirty Nails has been busy doing this week.

Parsnips

Parsnips are growing nicely, making good growth despite heavy losses to badgers in July. Dirty Nails has been using his own urine as a repellent, which seems to have done the trick. He has weeded and hoed through the crop, taking care not to damage the parsnip tops. Browned-off leaves have been thrown onto the compost heap. This not only keeps the crop clean, but also removes slug and snail hidey-holes.

Swedes

Swedes are beginning to fatten up. Some are cricket-ball sized. The odd plant has not grown and the small roots have turned to mush. Whilst weeding in the swede bed Dirty Nails has taken out all of these bad ones, as well as leaves from others that are yellowing. Keeping the crop healthy in this way is important, to keep the good swedes in peak condition. Being a member of the cabbage family, they are attractive to both the large and small white butterflies as food plants for their caterpillars. Dirty Nails checks for eggs, which he crushes, and caterpillars, which he carefully removes to nasturtiums grown as an alternative food plant elsewhere on the plot.

Scorzonera

Dirty Nails is pleased with his scorzonera. Judging from the lush crowns of long, spatula-shaped leaves, their elongated thong-like roots should be going down deep. Some scorzonera are sending up flower spikes. Dirty Nails cuts out these flowers. They resemble beautiful, ragged

NATURAL HISTORY IN THE GARDEN
House Martins

House martin numbers increase in August as fledglings take to the skies. Just sitting in the garden of a peaceful evening and gazing skywards provides stunning viewing of these lively, aerodynamic black and white birds. Their flight is both dashing and playful. Listen out for the house martins communicating with each other mid-flight, by way of a distinctive and friendly bubbling squeak.

dandelion heads on 2 foot (60 cm) stalks. Severed low down, this concentrates the plant's energy into the roots.

Salsify

At this time of year, rows of salsify look similar to leeks. They are a highly rewarding, low maintenance crop. Their tussocks of grey-green leaves are so massed that they are smothering out most weeds. The odd rogue thistle can be teased out by hand, or chopped off with a long handled hoe.

Root care

All these roots require little more than a watchful eye, and to be kept moist and weed-free throughout the coming autumn.

VEGETABLE SNIPPETS
OUT-OF-SEASON
PARSNIPS

It is not just foraging badgers that like to enjoy parsnips out of season. The home-producer can, too. For something different at this time of year, and as a taste of things to come, he might lift a bunch or two for a roasted treat. To give them that special sweetness, which only comes as a result of the first hard winter frosts, Dirty Nails pops the pale roots into his refrigerator for a couple or three days prior to cooking them up.

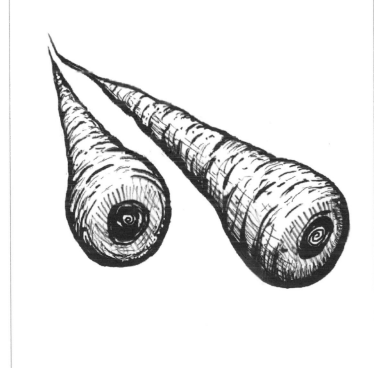

WINTER ONIONS

September, 1st Week

September is the month to plant winter onion sets. They are widely available and alternatively known as autumn onions. Dirty Nails gets consistently good returns with the Radar variety. They will tough out even the harshest winter, swell up in spring, and ripen for harvesting in late May. Winter onions do not store for very long, unlike main crops, but are valuable in early summer when stored main crop supplies are low or have been exhausted.

Onions like a sunny position and firm root-run. Dirty Nails prepares his onion bed a few days in advance of planting. He lightly forks over the selected plot and scatters handfuls of wood ash over it. He aims to dust the soil thinly but evenly. He rakes the bed level and to a crumbly tilth, then treads it down again before raking some more. The sets are planted at 6 inch (15 cm) intervals with a foot (30 cm) between rows.

Straight rows are much easier to look after than wonky ones, so Dirty Nails always uses a line of string tied between two sticks to mark them out. He makes a little planting nest for each one with his finger so as not to damage the acorn-sized miniature onion as he pushes it into the soil. Using both hands, he uses his thumbs and first-finger knuckles to secure each set, leaving the top of the bulb exposed. Sprouting roots can lift them out if they are not nestled in snugly. There is little else to do apart from keeping moist and weed-free, watch and wait.

For Dirty Nails growing veg is about so much more than just eating food. He

NATURAL HISTORY IN THE GARDEN
Slow Worm Babies

September is the prime month for slow worm babies to be born. Females hold their eggs internally until virtually the point of hatching, whereupon they deposit six to 12 fully developed youngsters in a thin, transparent shell that breaks open almost immediately. The 2 inch (5 cm) long, legless lizards are beautiful black and gold slivers of muscle the thickness of a knitting needle. Completely independent, they start feeding on tiny slugs straightaway.

completed his Radar onion planting in fabulous Indian summer weather, as a vast, shape-shifting gathering of house martins and swallows worked the insect-rich skies above. Being an active piece in the web of life, and feeling in tune with the rhythm of the seasons, is all part of the magic.

VEGETABLE SNIPPETS
THE PROS AND CONS OF USING PEAT

Peat is partially decomposed plant debris, and is located in bogs and moors. These are basically cool, water-logged environments. Taking thousands of years to form, peat is arguably the best growing medium for cultivating seedlings of a wide range of plants. It is stable, long lasting, well aerated, moisture retentive and an extremely popular choice in the greenhouse or shed as potting compost.

However the peat industry for horticultural purposes has been responsible for the destruction of 94% of British peat lands in the latter half of the twentieth century. These areas are, coincidentally, home to a range of rare or specialised plants and animals which are threatened by this habitat loss: wildlife such as sundews, butterworts and bladderworts (all carnivorous plants), nightjars (summer visiting relatives of the woodpecker) and many species of weird and wonderful insects.

There is also a global warming issue linked with peat extraction. Being plant matter, a vast amount of carbon is locked up in peat. When it is removed and used, this carbon is released into the atmosphere which enhances the greenhouse effect. The quantities of carbon contained herein, and potential damage caused by its liberation, should not be underesti-mated.

LEAF-MOULD AND COMPOST

This week Dirty Nails has emptied his compost and leaf-mould bins. He makes these containers cheaply and simply with old wooden pallets. These are set on end in a square and lashed together with strong wire. They are functional and well ventilated. He has his bins adjacent to each other so they can be easily worked together.

The leaf-mould is from last season's fall. Although it is not entirely broken down, it is rich, dark and crumbly. It is a lovely soil conditioner and good moisture retaining medium. Dirty Nails is an avid leaf collector during the autumn months and will scavenge the fallen bounty from almost everywhere and anywhere, except the sides of busy roads and woodlands. Roadside leaves are liable to be polluted and are best left alone. Those falling in wooded areas should be respectfully passed over also. They are an important part of the woodland cycle of life and death.

The compost bin has been filled with everything green over the last couple of years except potatoes and tomatoes (which are prone to carrying diseases), and particularly invasive weeds such as horsetail, bindweed and couch grass. Dirty Nails is always amazed to see how his compost heap can reduce from overflowing to half-full in a matter of days.

The leaf-mould is dug out first and wheelbarrow loads deposited on bare soil in the veg patch. The top

NATURAL HISTORY IN THE GARDEN
Ivy-leaved Toadflax

Dirty Nails is rather fond of a certain delightful little plant which adorns walls in the garden. It is ivy-leaved toadflax, and is a member of the figwort family that seeks a root-hold in cracks between stones and bricks. It tumbles out in straggly tufts. This is the end of a long flowering season which began in early summer.

Ivy-leaved toadflax sports dainty, pale purple flowers which are like miniature versions of the familiar garden snapdragon *Antirrinum* and, as the name suggests, has small ivy-shaped leaves. Once fertilised, this plant begins to physically curve its stems into the wall, pressing its tiny, ridged seeds into the cracks.

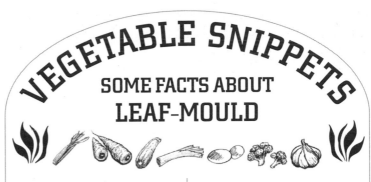

VEGETABLE SNIPPETS
SOME FACTS ABOUT
LEAF-MOULD

of the compost heap, which has not yet rotted, is removed into this space when it is empty. Underneath is a sweet smelling, fertile mixture which he spreads over the plot in piles also. As crops are cleared, Dirty Nails will cover bare soil with his home-made soil improving fertilisers, and leave until late winter. Then he will dig in the whole lot in preparation for another season of hopefully healthy and heavy-cropping home-grown produce.

Unlike green garden waste, which relies heavily on micro-bacteria to break it down into a wonderfully earthy compost, leaves utilise the rotting powers of fungi. Hence, leaf-mould is longer in the making, generally speaking, than compost. A heap of decomposing leaves should not be allowed to dry out, so dousing it with water may be necessary during a dry summer.

Leaf-mould is of only limited benefit when it comes to boosting nutrients in the soil. Apart from maintaining and enhancing the structure of the growing medium, and also its moisture retaining properties, the main virtue of leaf-mould is the role it plays in encouraging soil life. The largely invisible (to the naked eye) hordes of swarming microscopic and minute animals and fungi are an absolutely essential component of a fully functioning, healthy garden ecosystem.

Two words of caution, however – partially decomposed leaf-mould can rob nitrogen from the soil, and pine needles are strongly acidic so best avoided on the veg patch.

This bulky organic material can be easily made on a small scale with plastic bin bags. Simply fill a bag with leaves during the autumn, tie together at the top, stab a few holes in the sides for ventilation, and store out of the way somewhere. Forgotten about for a few months, the leaves will have transformed into a really useful mulch in a year or so.

WINTER PURSLANE AND CORN SALAD

Winter purslane

Claytonia, or winter purslane, is a pretty little plant that will provide succulent, fresh green leaves for use as a salad garnish during the winter months. Also known as miners' lettuce, in the past it was grown widely by working families as an important food source for when the days are short and the nights long.

Dirty Nails has been sowing winter purslane this week. He sprinkles the shiny, black pinhead-sized seeds over a tray of moist compost in much the same way as he applies a pinch of salt to a plate of food, and barely covers them with a fine layer of compost. The seed trays are put into the greenhouse to germinate. A cool windowsill is also ideal. The seeds require only to be kept moist and should start showing tiny shoots in a few days. They will grow on until large enough to handle, whereupon Dirty Nails will transplant them outside in rows at 4 inch (10 cm) intervals.

Once in the open air these autumn-sown plants are most productive when given the protection of a cloche covering. Individual leaves can be picked as soon as they are large enough, about the size of a two-pence piece. White flowers stem from the centre of round leaves which resemble a belly button. These are edible, too.

Winter purslane develops into a compact, low rosette of leaves which thrives on regular pickings. A dozen or more plants should provide sufficient greens to keep a family of four in

NATURAL HISTORY IN THE GARDEN
Blackbirds and Elderberries

Elderberries are swelling in darkening, ripening bunches that drip from the branches of the bushes dotted over the bank which backs on to Dirty Nails' plot. They are attractive to blackbirds. Watch out for flocks descending on the heavily laden plants this month. These handsome fellows like to cluck quietly to themselves as they gulp down a few berries, look up and around, shift position, and gobble up some more. Like most of the wildlife in the garden environment, the birds gorge themselves on nature's bounty during these heady days of plenty.

VEGETABLE SNIPPETS

SOME FACTS ABOUT
WINTER PURSLANE
AND CORN SALAD

fresh saladings throughout the dark months.

Corn salad

Corn salad, or lambs' lettuce, is another hardy vegetable which Dirty Nails grows for winter food. He broadcast-sows, or scatters, the small brown seeds on any spare patch of soil before raking them in. They will develop happily enough with or without a cloche, producing stout little plants. Leaves can be picked individually, but are a bit small. Dirty Nails prefers to tease out plants, dunk them in water to wash, trim the root, and present whole on a plate or in sandwiches.

Corn salad has a pleasant, nutty flavour and self-sows freely if a few are left to flower. Dirty Nails has it coming up, as if by magic, in various corners of the veg garden and it is always welcome.

Winter purslane

Winter purslane's other name, miners' lettuce, came about from the days of the American gold rush. In these frantic and sometimes desperate times, the fleshy leaves provided miners for gold with a crucial source of vitamin C. They actually depended on this low-growing plant to ward off scurvy. It is a good crop to cultivate in a partially sheltered spot, as this mimics its chosen natural habitat which would be shaded by trees.

Corn salad

Round about 1600 corn salad was introduced to the UK. It came from the Low Countries of northern Europe. The petite plant's alternative name, lambs' lettuce, refers to the fact that it is reputed to be at its greenest and most tender come the end of winter, which coincides with the traditional start of the lambing season.

As an escapee to the wild, in the UK it grows as a discreet plant that looks very much like a miniature forget-me-not. Corn salad prefers the dry soils provided by hedge banks and dunes. In places it may be a common weed of arable farmland.

RUNNERS, GREENS AND COMFREY

September, 4th Week

Runner beans

Dirty Nails has worked his runner beans hard and consistently since July. They have responded to his meticulous preparation and care magnificently, but now are virtually spent. He filled his trug for the last time this week before consigning them to the compost heap.

Dirty Nails always snips the stem just above ground level because there is a lot of nitrogen goodness in bean roots that will be returned to the soil as they decompose. Canes are then untied, pulled up, turned upside down, and the whole 6 feet (2 metres) or more of runner bean stem and leaf are slipped off in one go. There are always fat pods of beans, drying and dried, hidden away. Some of these can be saved for sowing next year.

Leaf beet and Swiss chard

Dirty Nails has been stripping his March-sown leaf beet and Swiss chard this week. He has removed all the big, tough outside leaves, leaving only a whorl of small, tender greenery. He carefully pulls the leaves, tugging downwards and sideways at once, or cuts them with a sharp knife. They should respond to this seemingly harsh treatment by growing more leaves for winter greens.

While the weather is mild they can be left as they are, but before the first cold snap Dirty Nails will mulch them thickly with straw or dry bracken to keep them cosy.

Comfrey

Comfrey continues to grow in abundance. Dirty Nails has cut his right back again and stuffed the leaves into an old wormery bin. He

NATURAL HISTORY IN THE GARDEN
Badgers in September

Badgers have had a busy month. They will have been fattening up for winter and high on their menu right now will be blackberries. This wild harvest grows abundantly all over. Finishing touches will be made to sett renovations or extensions. Dry grass and other vegetation are much sought after by badgers for bedding, and they will be collecting as much as they can to cosy-up their underground dwelling.

VEGETABLE SNIPPETS
AN EXPERIMENT WITH BEANS

keeps on top of his nettles too, which ensures a regular flush of fresh nettle tops. These are also put into the old wormery. Reward for this work is the potent liquid manure which will be strained off in early spring and used to feed all of next season's crops.

The difference between runner and French beans can be easily seen at seedling stage. In runners the bean splits open whereupon a shoot pushes up and out from within. The two bean halves are called cotyledons. They are the embryonic first seed-leaves (not true leaves at all) and remain underground after germination. French beans develop differently at this stage. As they respond to moisture the cotyledons arch up and out of the soil on top of a root shoot, then break apart to reveal the leaves inside.

Such quirks are easily demonstrated in a fun experiment for kids of all ages. By stuffing a jam jar full with damp (but not dripping) toilet paper or kitchen towels, and pushing a mix of three or four beans halfway down the sides against the glass, their progress can be followed. Subtle differences in germination can be observed and noted by the youngsters. A simple activity like this is fun, educational, and can have the added bonus of inspiring a lifelong interest in growing plants for future generations of budding gardeners.

SORTING OUT THE SHED

Throughout the hectic months of summer a whole array of useful bits and bobs, and a fair portion of useless articles too, gets stashed in the shed. Dirty Nails has been sorting out in here this week. It is a major job for him, and one that he tackles each spring and autumn. At this time of year it is prompted by the pressing need to create a handy space for stored potatoes, onions, squashes and other veg. These all need cool, frost-free conditions, and the pleasure in cooking home-grown produce is increased enormously if he can nip out to the shed on a dark evening and lay his hands on what he wants without fighting through a jungle of clutter first.

Getting the shed in good working order calms his whole being. If something needs doing, Dirty Nails can get to it with minimum fuss when he knows where to find the appropriate tool or piece of kit. Rolls of wire, offcuts of fleece, ropes, netting, sieves, pots and trays, bubble wrap, cloches, glass jars, fertilisers, carpet underlay, plastic bags, water carrying vessels, endless lengths of string and twine, bamboo canes, old newspapers, hoses, clothes pegs, squeezy bottles and much more, all do important jobs in the veg garden.

Dirty Nails has a place for everything, and everything in its place. He aims to store it all in an accessible and obvious manner. Tools can

NATURAL HISTORY IN THE GARDEN
Orb-Web (Diadem) Spiders

There are lots of spiders about at this time of year. Orb-web spiders are very much in evidence; the garden cross, or diadem, is one of 40 different species in Britain. It is these little beasties that spin the classic webs which hang as if festooned with a thousand glistening pearls on a dewy autumn morning, suspended between the skeletal stems of tall herbs and grasses which the thoughtful gardener leaves uncut around the plot margins.

Such silken snares are mostly made by females, who wait patiently in the centre until the vibrations of a trapped insect spur her into action and she pounces. She injects her hapless prey with a poison that paralyses the victim, but does not kill it straightaway. Then she wraps it in a purse of silk which keeps it fresh until she is ready to suck the body juices dry.

be cleaned and hoes sharpened. Broken trowels and rakes may be put to one side for repair later. A drop of oil to the moving parts of shears and secateurs can rejuvenate them. Dried seeds of favourite flowers can be sorted into old margarine tubs and laid out on a surface for further attention another time. He keeps the floor as clear as possible, his workbench swept and ready for action.

Dirty Nails wants his shed to be a quiet, peaceful oasis. He has a selection of choice reference books to dip into, and next year's seed catalogue to study and plan from. Connecting an electricity supply is something that Dirty Nails recommends. The combination of light, power, and order from chaos creates a beautiful space in which to potter away long evenings dreaming of what has been and what is to come.

VEGETABLE SNIPPETS

MULCHING IN
THE VEG PATCH

Applying a mulch to the veg patch, or areas of it, simply means using a material to cover the top layer of soil. This may be done for a number of reasons with both organic (natural) and inorganic (man-made) mulches.

The former include manure (FYM), leaf-mould, compost, grass mowings, or spent soil from pots and containers. These are substances which to a greater or lesser degree (and FYM is tops in this department) bulk up and feed the soil. They all encourage soil life, especially earthworms. These humble creatures are an absolutely essential component of healthy soil, playing a crucial role in incorporating and cycling matter, as well as helping drainage via their extensive and labyrinthine tunnels. An organic mulch may be used to keep the soil warm in winter, but cool in summer, prevent weeds from germinating by robbing them of the light, or conserve moisture if flopped down around a growing crop following a good soaking.

Newspaper and cardboard are considered as organic because they will rot down readily. They are especially useful when laid down underneath one of the mulches already mentioned, as a protective winter blanket.

Living mulches
'Living mulches' comprise growing a green manure to cover bare soil in gaps between cropping, or to protect the growing medium over winter from the erosive powers of wind and rain (not to be underestimated), especially on a slope. Legumes (the pea and bean family) such as clovers, lucerne (alfalfa) and field beans do a great job. They also fix atmospheric nitrogen in root nodules which is usefully exploited by the next batch of veggies grown on that piece. These, and others such as *phacelia,* also add a goodly supply of organic matter to soils when they are cut down and turned in before sowing.

Non-organic mulches
Non-organic mulches include black plastic sheeting, which is often left in place for a year or more to kill persistent weeds such as couch grass or dock by totally preventing light penetration. Land can still be worked with this sheeting in place by planting seedlings (or potato tubers) through carefully cut slits. Old carpet is another favourite amongst gardeners, as a light-excluding mulch used to suppress weeds and create bare soil without strenuous digging.

LOOKING AFTER PURPLE SPROUTING AND FROGS

Purple sprouting broccoli
Dirty Nails has been tending his purple sprouting broccoli this week. He always has a good rummage around the bottom of them at this time of year, clearing away dead and yellowing leaves to the compost heap, and weeding at the same time. They are by now fine plants with large leaves, a good crown and strong, thick stems. After this spruce-up they look magnificent and handsome.

Purple sprouting is a hungry brassica that likes to be bedded down in firm soil. To this end, Dirty Nails has been working hard. He has trodden the earth down around the base of each one with his heel, and applied a thick mulch of horse manure to the same area. He keeps a bucket and shovel in his vehicle, collecting manure from droppings on the road. He is thus able to keep a sack or two handy for this sort of job.

Lastly, Dirty Nails has staked each plant. A stout cane and baling twine are ideal for this purpose. Purple sprouting wants to grow quite large, 4 feet (120 cm) or more, and is susceptible to wind damage during gales. Good supports will hopefully prevent them from being rocked and having their roots loosened. Pigeon scarers in good working order are also vital. Made from compost bags cut into tassels and tied to tall canes, they move and rustle in the

NATURAL HISTORY IN THE GARDEN
Spindle Berries

During October Dirty Nails takes great pleasure in spotting colourful spindle bushes which grow just beyond the garden wall. They are full of colour at this time of the year, sporting dark red leaves and a stack of bright pink, four-lobed berries. When ripe these split open to reveal four orange seeds.

Spindle was ruthlessly cut out of the countryside by farmers in the years after World War 2 on account of the fact that the black bean aphid, so commonly seen on broad beans in the early summer, loves to hang out on spindle as an alternative host plant. A native to our shores, it is less out of favour these days, its wildlife and ornamental value being appreciated in these more environmentally enlightened times. Spindle wood is tough and hard, and the plant's name is a reminder of the common use it was put to in olden times, when weaving was an important job.

October, 2nd Week

breeze. There is little else to do now, except watch, wait and look forward to spring greens.

Frogs

Dirty Nails loves his frogs. They are second to none when it comes to pest control, feasting on all sorts of garden nuisances. Their soft croaking from the ponds on a warm evening is a natural, beautiful music. Whilst clearing away spent courgette plants, he disturbed one of his friends. The frog hopped away to behind the greenhouse where there is plenty of scope for hiding, safe from neighbourhood cats. Dirty Nails makes sure that his veg patch is frog-friendly by having lots of undisturbed places. Small piles of logs or stones that won't be moved, positioned strategically, ensure that the frogs are able to forage all areas of the plot with a safe hidey-hole always close by.

VEGETABLE SNIPPETS

SOME FACTS ABOUT BROCCOLI

A member of the cabbage tribe, purple sprouting broccoli heralds from Italy. The Romans adored this delectable vegetable. It was consumed in large quantities and with enthusiastic gusto at their infamously lavish and decadent banquets. By the early 1700s broccoli had been introduced to the UK, but at this time it was very much an unfamiliar novelty at mealtime.

There are many different varieties and strains of broccoli. The familiar purple sprouting described here is a long-standing plant, being sown in the spring, but not harvested until nearly a full year later. Calabrese is a quicker growing, summer-cropping variety (from a spring sowing also), and white sprouting is often confused with cauliflower.

All broccoli becomes tough if not cut and consumed when young. This is due to natural maturing processes within the plant, with internal sugars developing into fibre. Once this has occurred it is lost to the table as no amount of cooking and boiling will remedy the toughness.

The name broccoli comes from the Latin word *brachium*, which means strong arm. This is a reference to the sturdy, branching nature of this popular garden food plant.

AUTUMN-SOWN BROAD BEANS AND SUNDAY FEASTS!

Broad beans

This week Dirty Nails has been planting broad beans. Broads sown now come to fruition before a March planting. There are two big advantages to this. First, the more advanced autumn sowing is rarely attacked in late spring by broad bean Enemy Number One, the blackfly, because it has passed the vulnerable stage when these pests are on the loose. Secondly, the broad bean season is advanced by two or three weeks.

Several varieties of broad will over-winter quite happily, but Aquadulce is a particularly reliable and early cropper. If the winter turns very cold then they will appreciate protection via a horticultural fleece. Dirty Nails will be keeping his fingers crossed for a delicious and nutritious meal of autumn-sown broads before the end of May.

He prepares the plot first by weeding thoroughly, then digging in some fresh compost and raking level. At this time of year the soil is often quite damp, so he lays down wooden planks adjacent to where he wants to mark his rows, and works from these. The planks spread his body weight, minimising soil compaction, trampling and mess. Dirty Nails marks out the rows with canes and string, allowing 8 inches (20 cm) of space between. The thumbnail-sized beans are simply pressed into the fluffy soil to a depth of 3 inches (7 cm). This is slightly deeper than for spring-sown broads, but the extra snugness helps them to endure the worst of the winter weather. The beans are planted at 6 inch (15 cm) intervals. All being well, they should make a few inches of sturdy growth between now and New Year, then sit tight and wait for the spring rush.

Sunday feasts!

Dirty Nails usually has to loosen his trousers at the end of the week. Sunday is feast

NATURAL HISTORY IN THE GARDEN
Hibernating Small Turtoiseshell Butterflies

A few species of butterfly over-winter as adults. The small tortoiseshell commonly enters houses and sheds around now and settles with its wings folded together in a cool, quiet corner for the purpose of sleeping away the next few months. In this position the undersides of their wings disguise them as withered brown leaves. In the garden loose bark and the ivy-clad limbs of trees provide natural hibernation habitat for butterflies. Small tortoiseshells may over-winter communally.

Other hibernating species include the pale yellow brimstone and ragged-winged comma.

October, 3rd Week

VEGETABLE SNIPPETS

MEALTIME MAGIC

day for the family with many winter favourites now on the menu. A lot of work in the veg garden in the coming months will simply involve harvesting what is to be eaten on the day.

Lifting parsnips and other root veg for roasting cannot be hurried. Extracting a 1½ foot (60 cm) long scorzonera thong in one piece is a challenge, and an achievement in itself.

Swedes demand to be admired and their heady scent inhaled deeply before being washed, trimmed, peeled and cooked into a mash with spuds from store.

Leeks are in season from now until the end of March. Different varieties are cultivated to mature throughout both autumn and winter. Digging leeks for same-day consumption is a thrill in any weather. Fresh from the ground, they exude the most wonderful aroma. Being outside, trimming the roots and flag from a leek as dusk approaches, is about as good as it gets for Dirty Nails, second only to eating the bounty.

There is little which can compare with the pleasure to be had from sallying forth into kitchen-garden or down the allotment on a Sunday morning at this time of the year, and spending a good hour or so gathering the ingredients for a big meal. In the company of distant, peeling church bells and a quiet stillness which lends a timeless magic to the season of plenty, this is 'pottering' at its very best. Veggies fresh from the ground demand time to prepare, in the harvesting, rubbing, scrubbing and washing. This is an integral part of the fun. After admiring and considering what is to be eaten, bad bits must be removed and the produce readied for cooking. It cannot be rushed, in the same way that cultivating a tempting row of, say, swedes, is not a venture to be entered into in a hurry.

Dirty Nails is a busy man, and he always has been. 'Burning the candle at both ends', his mother used to say some years ago. But growing your own veg tempers this. It reins the home producer in to the natural rhythmic cycles of the seasons, working with forces which are so beautifully honed that careful planning and a little respectful forethought can reap plentiful rewards year-round. Sharing the bounty at mealtime, either with the children, with friends, or both, is a family ritual which has provided the household with some of its finest moments. There is nothing like a healthy hunger for good food to bring folk together.

ESSENTIAL GREENHOUSE WORK & POTTING-ON PURSLANE

The greenhouse
Cleaning and disinfecting the greenhouse is not a job that Dirty Nails looks forward to, but in the interests of continuing good crops, it has to be done. Diseases such as grey mould, or botrytis, thrive in the warm, enclosed conditions of the greenhouse environment. Their spores spread invisibly. These, and numerous other nasties, need to be cleansed in order to avoid future problems.

First thing is to remove the entire contents. Dirty Nails stacks all his kit on wooden pallets ready for sorting and washing later. By this time of year there are always lots of spiders that have taken up residence in the greenhouse. Dirty Nails attempts to catch and release every one before disinfecting begins. Most spiders will drop down on a silken thread from their corner when stroked with a fine brush, and can be caught in a container held below. It's a time-consuming and fiddly task, but one that is undertaken out of respect for these amazing hard-working little creatures.

Then it is a case of mopping-out and washing-down the whole greenhouse interior with a biodegradable disinfectant, diluted to the manufacturer's recommended ratio. Washing the contents is next. Dirty Nails only uses plastic pots and trays, which makes cleaning easier. His staging, which

NATURAL HISTORY IN THE GARDEN
Hogweed

In area of the plot left to go a bit wild, hogweed grows in abundance. It is a much maligned species and the sap can irritate the skin if the sun shines on it when still wet. Nonetheless, it is a vital source of sustenance for declining bumble bees. Having been in flower since June, displaying sturdy umbels of white flowers, this most common species of the parsley family is setting seed at the moment. The skeletal, saucer-sized platters hold clusters of disc-shaped seeds smaller than an old halfpenny. Heads held aloft on thick, browning stems, their ripe seeds scatter to the ground when disturbed by strong, gusting winds or are knocked by either gardener or foraging badgers.

October, 4th Week

can be built up and taken down as required, is plastic too. Disinfecting this is straightforward, using a large bucket of weak disinfectant to dunk everything into, with a toilet brush to dislodge caked-on potting compost and dirt.

It's an outside job and can be done little by little as and when equipment is needed for use. With a howling wind all around, leaves doing the manic dance of the autumn fall, and temperatures low, it can feel thankless and tiresome. But when the gales subside and warm late-season rays catch his cheeks and warm his shoulders, Dirty Nails is in his heavenly element. Sitting on a stool, sleeves rolled up, sloshing and scrubbing mucky old pots which have raised all manner of veggies over the last few months, is an honest and wholesome task.

Winter purslane

The winter purslane, which was sown indoors during mid-September, is large enough to be potted on. Four inch (10 cm) pots are prepared by filling with potting compost and pushing a hole in the middle about 2 inches (5 cm) deep to accommodate the roots. Dirty Nails loosens the seed tray soil by gently tearing out a clump of seedlings, taking utmost care not to damage roots or stalks. By holding the long oval leaves, he patiently teases the seedling purslane plants apart and selects the biggest and strongest for potting on. Their straggly roots are lowered into the prepared pots. Compost is lovingly pressed down to snuggle them in. They are now ready to go into the newly cleaned greenhouse.

Kept moist, they should be growing fleshy round leaves enough to commence harvesting in a few weeks.

GARLIC

November, 1st Week

Now is the perfect time to plant garlic for over-wintering. It is a tough member of the onion tribe and a fairly reliable cropper as long as the ground is not too heavy. Dirty Nails has been planting his garlic cloves this week. It is a pretty straightforward task, and as with most veg the preparation is all important. He cleans the bed completely of weeds, and gives it a thorough dusting with dry wood ash. This is dug in, and raked to a fine and fluffy tilth. The bed is now ready.

Garlic can be planted at this time of year, or in early spring. Dirty Nails is careful about choosing the right variety for the right time of year. He selects Messidrome and the purple-tinged Germidour for a late autumn sowing, varieties that are bursting to sprout soon if they have not already begun to do so. Other types such as Printador, that don't show green shoots until March or April, should be planted in the early spring.

Bulbs are prised gently apart, and individual cloves separated. Each one of these will hopefully grow into a complete bulb for harvesting next June or July. Dirty Nails places the cloves on top of the soil in blocks rather than lines, with 5 inches (13 cm) between each one. When all the cloves are in position he firmly plunges them, one at a time, down into the earth, pointed end uppermost, to a depth of 2½ inches (6 cm) and smoothes over. A cold spell immediately after planting is to be hoped for

NATURAL HISTORY IN THE GARDEN
Wall Pellitory

Wall pellitory is a common plant in Dirty Nails' neighbourhood, jutting out from walls and cracks in stonework. It thrives all over the south west, wherever construction work by humans provides a suitable niche away from its favoured natural cliff and rocky outcrop habitats.

In November wall pellitory is a tufty, straggly plant, with elongated diamond-shaped green leaves borne on reddish stems. In mild weather it may still be flowering, displaying tiny pink blooms in clusters at the junction of leaf and stem. A cousin of the stinging nettle, it is an alternative food source for some of our aristocratic summer butterflies.

VEGETABLE SNIPPETS

SOME FACTS ABOUT
GARLIC

as this stimulates the garlic into dividing and developing strong roots. Shoots should be showing well by New Year. All that is required is to keep weed-free.

Garlic is a powerful little plant, well liked and consumed with great gusto in the Dirty Nails household. Breaking up and planting four or five bulbs now, and again in the spring, is more than enough to give his family of four a home-grown garlic aroma all year round.

Originating in the Middle East, garlic as we know it is descended from wild stock and was developed by selective breeding way, way back long ago. It has been grown in Britain since before 1548 and is used in cooking as a flavour enhancer. Garlic (*Allium sativum*) is a particularly good foil for onions, tomatoes and ginger.

Endowed with a long and celebrated history in both culinary and medical fields, garlic is considered by many to be a natural tonic on account of the many health promoting virtues with which it is credited.

The potent garlic aroma associated with its consumption occurs when any of the plant cells are damaged. Violation via chopping, crushing or chewing prompts enzymes within the cells into a reaction. This is where the distinctive smell comes from. It is possible that this naturally occurring phenomenon evolved in garlic to counter grazing by herbivorous (plant-eating) animals.

Traditionally, complete bulbs (or heads) of garlic were hung up around doorways and chimney-breasts in the home to ward off evil spirits. Similarly, to keep vampires at bay, a clove or two was kept in a pocket about one's person.

WINTER WORK AND HARVESTING JERUSALEMS

Winter work

Dirty Nails has been doing a lot of general tidying-up jobs in the veg garden this week. Removing dead leaves from crops, clearing patches of weeds that are beginning to try their luck, and sorting out piles of canes, are all important jobs to do. Other jobs are removing places for slugs, snails, and other pests to lurk, and allowing easy access to the soil for robins and blackbirds. These birds are ever watchful for pests that do venture out.

Working out next year's crop plan begins now. Dirty Nails finds it easier to visualise what he wants to do when the plot is clearly defined. To this end he has been busy clearing the edges. The calendula, or pot marigold, which he grows to suppress invasive couch grass, are all but finished now. He has been pulling spent plants up and chucking them onto the compost heap. He burns the rest of the weeds along the edge. There are always a few rogue lengths of couch, and lots of splinters of horsetail, in amongst them. Their presence can ruin a good compost heap.

As he cleans the edge, Dirty Nails throws the soil inwards, creating a shallow trench. Apart from being pleasing to look at, it will mark where the pot marigolds will be sown next spring, from seed saved this summer.

Jerusalem artichokes

Jerusalem artichokes come into season at this time of year. Dirty Nails cuts his plants down to about 6 inches (15 cm) now. The top growth is thick and woody so he reduces it to short lengths before it goes on the compost. Underground, large knots of gnarled and twisted tubers have formed. They demand to be dug up with care, as even a tiny piece of tuber will grow again if left in the soil. One plant is harvested at a time, and the crop stored in a box of

NATURAL HISTORY IN THE GARDEN
Badgers in November

Badgers are less active this month. There are fewer feeding opportunities, especially if frosty weather sets in. They slow down their foraging and social activity in order to conserve vital energy and fat stores during the bleak weeks ahead.

November, 2nd Week

compost until needed.

Anything a potato can do, a Jerusalem can do too. However Dirty Nails advises against eating huge amounts at any one sitting. Although they have a delectable, distinctive and unusual creamy taste and texture, over-indulgence can cause tummy troubles for some people.

VEGETABLE SNIPPETS
FARTICHOKES!

Jerusalems contain a carbo-hydrate called inulin. Unlike other types of starch, such as those found in spuds for instance, inulin is not absorbed by the body, and thus not utilised as an energy. A few folk have a slight intolerance to it and because of this, inulin can start to ferment inside the guts. Hence the tendency in some to suffer flatulence after partaking in the consumption of said veg. It is this quality that makes Jerusalems legendary around the dinner table, especially with the children. Due to these wind-breaking properties it is dubbed fartichoke, much to the amusement of the giggling kids, but not a frowning Mrs Nails.

SUNFLOWERS, TEASELS AND FINCHES

As the cold weather really sets in, Dirty Nails finds great pleasure in watching the birds that visit his garden for a feed. As well as providing nuts and other tidbits for his feathered friends, he always cultivates certain plants especially for the birds.

Sunflowers

Sunflowers are good to grow. At this time of year thick stalks of the Giant Single variety still stand 10 feet (3 metres) or more. Their large heads, which at the peak of the season were incredible gold and brown glories the size of a dinner plate, are now drooping, dark and pecked ragged. They are high up on the menu for many seed eaters, including greenfinches. Dirty Nails will leave his sunflowers standing right through the winter, unless adverse weather snaps them first.

To please his eye in the summer, and feed the birds in winter, he sows sunflowers singly in pots of moist compost during March, popping in the black and white striped seeds to a depth of ½ an inch (1½ cm). They are strong growers in the greenhouse or on the windowsill and should be big enough to plant out in early May. Allowing 2 feet (60 cm) or more at this stage may seem a bit extravagant, but Dirty Nails is always generous with his sunflowers when it comes to giving them space. They like to be kept watered during dry spells, and respond to a monthly dose of nettle and comfrey feed with energetic growth and spectacular flowers from high-summer onwards.

Teasels

Another provider of nourishment for birds in winter is the teasel. By November it has become a crisp brown skeleton, up to 6

NATURAL HISTORY IN THE GARDEN
'Jenny' Wren

Look out for the diminutive wren this month. With woody plants now all but bare, these stumpy little birds can be spotted as they flit between trees and bushes around the garden. Wrens are less than 4 inches (10 cm) in length and sport chestnut-brown upper parts with lighter colouration below. A bandit-like eye stripe is distinctive, and so too the short, cocked tail. They are active, like clockwork toys, constantly bobbing up and down as they tick-tack along branches in search of insect food. Wrens have a powerful song and at this time of year listen out for their short, sharp, 'tit-tit-tit' delivery. It is slightly harsher than the not dissimilar robin.

November, 3rd Week

feet (2 metres) tall, with numerous stems supporting dozens of spiky, egg-shaped seed heads. It is a magnet for goldfinches. These birds have beaks which are perfectly evolved to fit into the depths of these 'hedgehogs' and extract the seeds. A flock of goldfinches is known as a charm, and when travelling thus they have a beautiful call which makes Dirty Nails think of thick and precious dripping liquid. His veg patch has teasels popping up all over the place, descendants of those that he introduced from a packet of mixed wildflower seeds. They develop a low rosette of leaves, studded with soft spikes, and are easy to identify.

Dirty Nails moves these self-sown plants to his chosen growing site any time from October to March. Borne on the 'hedgehog' in high summer, the purple flowers are also very attractive to many long-tongued insects.

VEGETABLE SNIPPETS

FULLER'S TEASEL

Both the common teasel and fuller's teasel are valuable additions to the rough corners of a vegetable patch, or integrated into the flower border. Their wildlife value in terms of attracting pollinating insects is excellent. Subsequently the seeds are attractive to birds. The plants themselves are physically impressive. They lend an air of majestic structure to a garden, especially if allowed to stand throughout the winter when they can become beautifully decorated with frost.

Teasels are easy to grow in all soils (including heavy clay) as long as their position is a sunny one. They self-seed freely, and in subsequent years will need to be kept in check with regular weeding sessions to remove the flat rosettes of tough green leaves sported by immature seedlings. This is not too demanding because as first-year youngsters they send down a creamy central tap-root which is lifted easily enough when loosened with the aid of a border fork.

Fuller's teasel differs from the common variety in that the seeded flower head develops hooked barbs as opposed to spikes which are straight. This quality was exploited initially during the agricultural depression from 1650 to 1750 in areas such as North Somerset, where fuller's teasel became an important crop. The dried seedheads were employed in the woollen industry for raising the nap on manufactured cloth.

Fuller's teasel has its reputed medicinal uses too. Ointments made from the roots were used to treat warts. An infusion of dried root was believed to be beneficial to one's stomach, to enhance one's appetite and clean the liver.

IN THE VEG STORE & PUTTING GLOBE ARTICHOKES TO BED

A cold and wet weekend is an ideal time to get into the vegetable store. Veggies kept under cover in a frost-free place require regular inspections, and anything going rotten or 'on the turn' must be either discarded to the compost (except potatoes, which should be binned) or used immediately. Dirty Nails keeps a keen eye on his stash of stored winter veg via thorough monthly check-ups. He handles everything, turning and pressing gently.

Garlic, shallots and onions
Garlic and shallots are fairly reliable storers, although uneaten winter garlic varieties could be starting to sprout. A handful of shallots may go soft and need removing from storage trays. Red onions are much poorer storers than main crops and should be on the menu regularly until supplies are gone. They are wonderful roasted, caramelised or raw, and their seasonality simply amplifies their deliciousness. Some main crop onions get chucked at each checking. Dirty Nails gets rid of any gone soft or showing green shoots, and is ever-watchful around their roots. The odd one rots from here, oozing a reddish-brown slime that hollows out the middle. Early detection is vital as the dripping goo may contaminate other onions and smells appalling.

NATURAL HISTORY IN THE GARDEN
Redwings and Fieldfares

Over-wintering thrushes are in the area about now. Redwings and fieldfares breed in northern Europe and Scandinavia, but journey to the warmer climes out of season, where the living is not so harsh. Redwings are brown on top with a red sash along their flank and under the wing. At 10 inches (25 cm), fieldfares are nearly 2 inches (5 cm) larger than their cousins, and display slate-grey heads and rumps with a rusty brown back and dark tail. Both species show classic thrush-mottled breasts.

They like to feed communally, scrounging around the country larder for hawthorn berries and windfall apples. Flocks may be heard at night-time passing overhead, keeping in close contact via plaintive, hissing calls.

November, 4th Week

These losses are inevitable. It is always sad to condemn any food crops, especially after lovingly tending them through the summer and making every effort to provide the best storage conditions. But Dirty Nails takes heart nevertheless, as every rotten onion removed prolongs the keeping quality of the others, and he cultivates enough to withstand these losses.

Potatoes

Potatoes demand to be smelled as well as handled. Those in sacks can suffer heavy losses if just one spud rots and it spreads. A deep inhalation, head down in the sack, is what Dirty Nails does. He knows from experience that he'll sniff out a rotten spud if there is one, because the unforgettable smell is truly ghastly. In spite of meticulous preparation, washing and drying, avoiding heavy losses is all part of the fun! If the veg store develops any unusual aroma, check the tatties first. Those stored one-deep in plastic fruit trays are far easier to check, but must be kept in the dark. Coats draped over the tray stack is a good option.

Squashes

Squashes store differently according to variety. Dirty Nails has always struggled to stop his butternuts from going mouldy much beyond this time of year. If a failing butternut is caught early, most of it can be saved if eaten at once. It is a fantastic ingredient for winter-warmer soups. Acorn and spaghetti squashes, and other thick-skinned orangey and bluish onion-shaped types store for far longer. With luck they could be fine well into New Year and saved until the other varieties have been eaten.

Globe artichokes

Outside, globe artichokes don't relish severe weather. With this in mind Dirty Nails has put his to bed for the winter. He cuts down fresh growth to about 8 inches (20 cm) and applies a thick mulch of leaves around the base of the plant, but not over the crown. On top of this he criss-crosses twigs and sticks, then one or two layers of horticultural fleece which is pegged down and held with heavier planks of wood. This should keep the globes nice and cosy even in extreme conditions, but still allow air to circulate and prevent the crown from rotting.

This job was undertaken in biting cold and persistent heavy rain, in stark contrast to the beautiful, hot conditions of midsummer, when the heads are fat and ready for cutting. These extremes really are the spice of life for Dirty Nails who loves being out in the weather whatever it is up to.

WINTER DIGGING

November, 5th Week

This week Dirty Nails has started to dig over his vegetable plot. His aim is to turn over every vacant piece of soil during the next couple or three months. Much of the ground is growing a green manure crop. He takes the hoe to this, cutting it all down then digging it in. The goodness in the plants is released into the soil as they decompose. Elsewhere, leaf-mould and compost mulches were applied in the autumn. They too will be dug in.

Although there are many schools of thought on the merits of digging in relation to growing vegetables, Dirty Nails always rough-digs his patch in the winter. He favours this regime for many reasons, which all ultimately lead to the production of wholesome, delicious food. Digging the soil to a depth of one spit (the length of a spade

head) exposes it to the winter elements. A freshly dug piece of ground looks like a still-life of choppy waters at sea. By springtime this will have been weathered by the forces of rain, wind and frost into a calmer, smoother picture. The resulting friable soil is easily turned into a seedbed when spring sowing time comes around again.

Dirty Nails knows that he willl be able to manage the rush of work much more easily if he has prepared the ground well in advance. He also relishes the closeness of his rela-tionship with the earth as he digs. Winter digging is part of this ongoing partnership. With a tender, loving and careful approach year on year, he works with the soil and continually renews his acquaintance with it.

Friendly robins are almost constant companions at this time.

They drop in fearlessly, hopping from clod to clod, stopping, tilting their heads to one side listening, and then diving into a crack or hollow to snaffle a tasty morsel. Robins find rich pickings where the ground is disturbed, and account for many soil pests at the same time. Dirty Nails enjoys digging most when in the company of these beady-eyed little birds. They give him an excuse to take regular pauses, straighten his back and survey the work in progress.

Digging is a strenuous activity and it is easy to get lost in the rhythmic meditation of the job, which can lead to backache the next day. Dirty Nails seldom digs for more than half an hour before taking a break and doing something else. Each turn of sod is a labour of love, undertaken slowly, methodically and with respect. He keeps his back as straight as possible, letting his knees, thighs and arms take the strain.

Working on wet ground is extra hard work and can do more harm than good by compressing the soil structure. If great clods are sticking to the boots, then it is too wet to dig. Where the ground is sloping, backache can be minimised by working along the contour facing uphill. With a sensible and realistic approach to digging his sizeable veg plot, Dirty Nails hopes to be able to tackle this annual task manually for many years to come.

VEGETABLE SNIPPETS
SOIL
ORGANIC MATTER (SOM)

Soil organic matter (SOM) is any part of the soil that once lived. From both plants and animals, it is dead stuff in varying degrees of decomposition. SOM is highly nutritious and therefore an essential ingredient in the production of home-grown veggies. It is, however, only a small component of most garden soils in this country, comprising just 2% to 5% of the good earth that most of us have to play with.

When rotted to the maximum, SOM is called humus. It is dark brown, allows easy passage of water (is porous), spongy to touch and has a rich smell. It is in this state when most of its nutrients are available to crops.

Another key element of SOM is the part it plays in a healthy structure. By opening up the land, it introduces plenty of oxygen. It provides a great habitat and high source of energy for creatures living in this domain, from earthworms to microbes. These all have a crucial role to play in the well-being of the veg plot.

It is also fantastic for conditioning soils. When heavy and/or compacted, and difficult to work, SOM makes the soil more friable and much easier going. Where the growing medium is too light and/or free-draining, SOM binds particles together which gives the soil bulk and body.

SOM does, however, have its limitations. Garden compost can harbour plant viruses and/or diseases if infected material has been added to the refuse heap instead of being burnt. Similarly, perennial weed seeds can survive humification, and will germinate when compost is applied to the plot.

Farmyard manure must be well-rotted lest it give off ammonia, while fresh straw and leaves can rob the soil of nitrogen as they rot down, which can cause a nutrient imbalance. They should be partially decomposed at the very least when incorporated into the ground.

TENDING WINTER ONIONS

December, 1st Week

This week Dirty Nails has been busy in his winter onion bed. The Radar onions which he planted as sets in September have taken well. Their healthy greenery on top indicates strong rooting down below, which is vital for a heavy crop. At this time of year the onions have settled down and won't make any visible growth for a while. It's the perfect opportunity to get in amongst them and have a good tidy up.

Dirty Nails likes to weed on his hands and knees between the rows first. The weeds are not far past the seedling stage and have tenacious roots. They need to be teased out whole. A kitchen fork is used to gently extract them from the damp soil. He works slowly forwards along the rows like this, filling a bucket with young weeds as he goes. The bed soon cleans up, and the onions show off handsomely in their lines. With this job done, Dirty Nails employs his hoe. He hoes carefully, moving backwards, pushing and pulling the blade back and fore, roughing up the soil surface and disturbing any tiny weeds that are just germinating. This is a job that Dirty Nails thoroughly enjoys, not least because it feels so satisfying to be genuinely weeding and hoeing in December.

All members of the onion family appreciate the goodness contained in wood ash. Radars are no exception. Dirty Nails will be sprinkling down and hoeing in a top dressing of wood ash during early spring. To this end he saves and stores all ash from home fires and bonfires, which needs to be kept dry prior to use.

NATURAL HISTORY IN THE GARDEN
Badgers in December

Female (sow) badgers may have held fertilised eggs in their bodies since last spring, but now is the time when amazing internal processes cause the egg to become implanted in the womb. Usually litters comprise two or three cubs, to be born any time from mid-January to the end of March.

VEGETABLE SNIPPETS

WOOD ASH

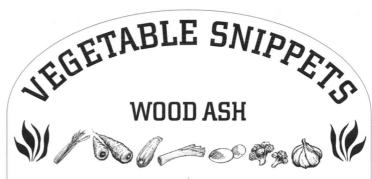

Wood ash is a useful by-product of bonfires in the garden. Having a regular burn-up is an important job. Fires cleanly and effectively get rid of diseased plant material, and deal with troublesome weeds such as thick-rooted dandelions, persistent creeping buttercup, and the seemingly impossible-to-kill trio of bindweed, couch grass and horsetail. Dirty Nails loves standing beside a crackling blaze, warming his hands, absorbing the deliciously romantic aroma of wood smoke into his clothes and hair. Fire is a magical, elemental force, and although not quite living it is nonetheless very much alive. In no time fire transforms harmful waste into a valuable resource which will do the veggies no end of good.

Wood ash is almost pure potash. This is beneficial to all crops in varying degrees. Sugary and starchy veg demand it to help their metabolism. For instance, spuds love it when sprinkled between the rows as a top dressing prior to earthing them up in the summer. Potash is high in potassium which is a nutrient that encourages flowering and fruiting. Hence it is good for beans, curcubits (squashes, marrows, cucumbers and the like), tomatoes and others that set a fruiting crop. Dirty Nails shakes a handful around the base of these plants when they are coming to this stage of their lives.

A week or so before sowing, wood ash is applied to a prepared seedbed at the rate of about one heaped trowel per square yard (1 square metre). It will be appreciated by the developing seedlings.

WASPS, LEAF-MOULD AND BRASSICAS

Wasps and leaf-mould

Dirty Nails had a very pleasant surprise this week, regarding leaf-mould. Throughout the summer months one of his leaf-mould bins was squatted in by wasps. To begin with their hectic activity was a bit of a worry. However gardener and insects lived happily in the same space. Dirty Nails took care to always work slowly, quietly and deliberately, so as not to disturb the nest when working in close proximity. He spent much time watching the wasps in their daytime toil, lifting out from and dropping into a small hole at the back of the leaf pile. The relationship was mutually beneficial. In return for being left in peace, the colony of up to 2,000 wasps accounted for countless insect pests including aphids and caterpillars, which they need to feed their larvae. In fact they kept a dozen purple sprouting plants growing immediately adjacent to the nest completely free of cabbage white caterpillars all summer long.

The cold weather of winter eventually killed off the drone and worker wasps, and hopefully the fertilised queen crept away to somewhere safe for hibernation. What they left was access to 15-month old leaf-mould, beautifully decomposed to a soft, crumbly texture. Rather than spread this onto the veg plot for digging in, Dirty Nails has decided to use it as the finest quality potting compost. To this end, he has shovelled the growing

NATURAL HISTORY IN THE GARDEN
Blue Tits

Look out for blue tits. These 4½ inch (12 cm) long, lively little blue and yellow customers with white faces are a familiar sight amongst the trees and scrubby slopes behind Dirty Nails' garden. In the winter months they often flock together with other species such as chaffinches, nuthatches, great and coal tits. A meagre ration is eked out communally. Blue tits hunt amongst tree branches, searching for insects and spiders in nooks, crannies and under loose bark. They often dangle acrobatically upside-down in order to get at a tasty morsel.

December, 2nd Week

medium into old plastic compost and bark chipping bags and is transferring them into the greenhouse ready for use. Well rotted leaf-mould is perfect for sowing seeds into. For potting on seedlings Dirty Nails will mix the leaf-mould with molehill soil to a ratio of 50/50.

Brassicas

All brassicas, including purple sprouting broccoli, have had attention lavished on them this week. Dirty Nails has trodden down the soil around the base of their stems and refastened supporting canes. Yellowing bottom leaves are constantly being picked off and cleared away to keep the plants as clean and healthy as possible. All the cabbage family are gross feeders and have a thick mulch of well rotted manure applied around the firmed-in stem bases.

VEGETABLE SNIPPETS

A BRIEF HISTORY OF ALLOTMENTS

The history of allotments dates back to at least 1066, and the feudal system established by William the Conqueror. In those long-ago days ruling gentry lorded it over their serfs who were allowed to cultivate strips of land in the open manorial fields, alongside meadow and grazing rights. Field enclosures in the 1500s removed some of these rights. A hundred-odd years later, slave-driven workers had been reclassified as peasants. As part of their meagre ration, they were permitted to grow foodstuffs next to their tied cottages (known as pottagers).

The next wave of enclosure occurred between 1760 and 1818. Open and common land was grabbed on an enormous scale. During that time 5,000 Acts of Parliament secured seven million acres into private ownership. A further 17 million acres were simply taken, principally by the landed gentry and yeoman farmers. Peasants were now the 'labouring poor'. Some parish and private ground was rented out to those folk for veg production, but opposition to the needs of the workers was rife. Consequently, land allotted for such purposes was few and far between. Where it did exist, strict rules applied. For instance, in some places gardening was prohibited on weekdays between 6 am and 6 pm, and all day Sunday.

Laws were passed in 1845 to legally secure cheap and accessible allotments. Although the motives were arguably to keep the working classes out of the pub when not slogging away for someone else, this was a momentous change. Allotments of a practical size for purpose became established and popular, especially in urban areas. In 1919 and 1945, immediately following the two World Wars, well over a million allotments were actively in service. The radical societal and land-use changes since then have seen much 'leisure garden' space lost to development schemes and disuse, but statutory regulations demand that authorities provide these areas for use by the Council Tax-paying public. Modern sites are havens for people of all races, ages, genders, political persuasions and classes: individuals who seek solace in the company of the soil and what it can produce.

Enthusiasm for allotment gardening comes and goes like most fads and fashions. The first thing to do if the prospect takes your fancy is to visit the local council offices, enquire, and (more than likely) put your name on a waiting list. Depending on the mood of the day, an opportunity to get deep down and dirty may come along sooner than you think. Be prepared!

SHALLOTS

December, 3rd Week

This week Dirty Nails has been planting shallots. This prolific and reliable member of the onion tribe is traditionally planted on the shortest day of the year and harvested on the longest. Although the crop is not always ripe for lifting on 21 June, Dirty Nails likes to get his shallots in the ground on midwinter's day. He selects the best of last season's crop, those that are firm, whole and about an inch (2½ cm) or so across, for planting now. These are descendants of shallots which a friend gave to him some years ago, and this annual Winter Solstice ritual has kept them on the menu ever since.

Shallots are sun-lovers, and this fact is considered when a growing site is chosen. Dirty Nails cleans the plot meticulously prior to planting, and lightly forks over the soil as he does this. A liberal dusting of dry wood ash is applied and raked in. Because shallots prefer to grow in firm ground, he treads it down with small sideways steps all over. The bed is then given one more light raking before receiving the shiny brown bulbs. All loose, flaky outer skin and stalk should be carefully rubbed or cut off before they are planted at 9 inch (23 cm) intervals, in rows a foot (30 cm) apart.

Dirty Nails ties string between two canes to keep his planting lines straight. These are easy to maintain

NATURAL HISTORY IN THE GARDEN
Foxes

From the silent depths of a long cold night, listen out for the unearthly screaming wails of foxes. This primeval noise is the female (vixen) calling out to potential mates in the vicinity. The mating season occurs from December until February, and during this time the male (dog) foxes travel extensively over large areas of town and country looking for a suitable partner.

Once contact has been established the couple spend many days by each other's side. The dog will follow the vixen as if in a spell, and may be seen doing so even in broad daylight. After three weeks or so mating takes place many times. The foxes may become so embroiled in their business that they become locked together and oblivious to what is going on around them.

weed-free with a hoe. He makes a little planting nest with his thumb, and presses each set in gently to half its depth. The soil is then firmed back around the set with thumb and first finger, using both hands.

Shallots need to be inspected regularly for a couple of weeks after planting, until their roots have taken anchor. Cats, birds and frost can all lift them out of position, as can the growing roots if merely pushed into the ground and not nestled down securely. During his daily rounds Dirty Nails firms any sets that are showing signs of looseness.

All being well, they should be showing green shoots in a few weeks. Apart from the initial care and attention during rooting, shallots require only to be kept moist and weed-free in order to give a really big return for the space occupied.

VEGETABLE SNIPPETS
A BRIEF HISTORY OF
SHALLOTS

Shallots are part of the onion family, which boasts 450 species worldwide. This veg was a staple foodstuff in ancient Egypt. Shallots were introduced to European palates as *eschallots* in the twelfth century by returning Crusaders. Their onion-like bounty heralded from the ancient Palestinian (Canaan) city of Ascalon, from where they were believed to have originated.

MULCHING WITH BRACKEN

December, 4th Week

The threat of harsh weather and frozen ground is ever present at this time of year. Freezing conditions are both good and bad. Good, because the cold kills off a lot of soil borne pests, and because the action of freeze/thaw leaves previously dug soil loose and friable in the spring. But frozen ground can also be a problem when it comes to lifting roots and other crops that are still standing on the plot. Dirty Nails tries to minimise the risk of having much needed food crops locked in to frozen earth by applying a thick mulch. Straw or bracken is ideal for this purpose.

Dirty Nails uses bracken on account of it being freely available on areas of common land locally, and because it costs nothing to cut and gather apart from the time and effort. He uses shears for cutting low down, and then rakes it into piles before stuffing it into plastic bags. Even damp and rotting bracken has a lot of sharp, woody splinters. These can slice the fingers painfully, similar to a paper-cut, so Dirty Nails always wears gloves for this job.

Once in amongst his veg, he spreads the bracken thickly over parsnips, salsify, scorzonera and Jerusalem artichokes. Lines of 'snips may have to be marked with canes, but the others have enough tops to show their position amongst the cosy bedding.

NATURAL HISTORY IN THE GARDEN
Cotoneaster Berries

There are many different types of cotoneaster. They are red-berried trees or shrubs with glossy green leaves. The abundant crop they carry in the winter months is often left untouched until late in mild seasons, but could prove to be a lifesaver for blackbirds and other berry-eaters in prolonged cold weather.

This final month of the year is the perfect time for lingering in the garden. For Dirty Nails there is always something to stimulate the senses and lift the heart, be it massive, drifting cloudscapes, intricate patterns traced by bare-stemmed tree branches, the chattering machine-gun rattle of a handsome magpie, or any amount of nature's wonders.

VEGETABLE SNIPPETS
BRACKEN USE THROUGH HISTORY

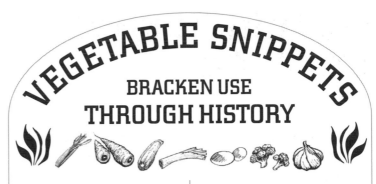

Leeks are essential eating right now. To ensure access in even really hard weather, Dirty Nails mulches around their bases and between rows.

These can be tough times for the birds which afford such wonderful year-round company in the garden. A few handfuls of mixed seeds, scattered along paths and away from cat danger, are always well appreciated by his feathered friends.

Since Neolithic times, some 3000 BC, bracken has been put to a multitude of uses by humans. Dried bracken makes excellent litter for livestock. The Romans thought of it so highly that they used it as bedding for themselves as well as their animals. It has been commandeered as fuel for heating purposes, and the baking and brewing processes. Bracken was widely employed in the construction of dwellings, especially for thatching. As compost in the gardens of large estate houses, well-rotted bracken was used as a bulky conditioning material which both lightened up heavy soil and bulked up light soils.

Latterly, in the 1800s, it was used for the production of potash. In this form it was an integral part of early industrial processes including glass and soap making, as well as the manufacture of detergents. Throughout this time bracken continued to be widely burnt for domestic purposes also.

Nowadays quantities may be mechanically harvested, allowed to decompose, then bagged up and sold in garden centres under various names including forest bark. Many authorities consider that there is now too much of this plant growing in the UK. One theory for the explosive spread of bracken in many areas is that, now it is seldom utilised and therefore cut less, rotting fronds act as a protective 'self-mulch' over the tender crowns in winter. Instead of getting nipped in the bud during freezing cold spells, it is surviving and thriving. As a resource for the gardener, it is widely available for the taking.

PLANNING FOR THE SEASON AHEAD

January, 1st Week

With the arrival of a new year Dirty Nails gets busy planning his planting schedule for the coming season. He already has most of the seeds in hand, having placed an order with a reputable and reliable company over the phone a few weeks ago. Anything overlooked then can be easily mailed to him with a call.

Dirty Nails is a meticulous note-taker, and at times like this his scribblings are invaluable for plotting out what to plant and when. Writing down a planting plan, month-by-month for the whole year, keeps tasks in proportion and under control. He is clearly able to see how his veg garden will develop. As each month rolls along, he sorts out the seeds that he will be handling for those four-odd weeks. This careful attention to detail gets him in the mood for what lies ahead, and ensures that when the really manic seed-sowing months of March, April and May arrive, he is not overwhelmed by jobs to do. Weather conditions will affect planting times. Wet or cold spells can force the postponement of sowing certain crops, especially those sown outside, direct into the soil. Flexibility is needed and an instinctive ability to seize the right moment for the right job.

Dirty Nails never grows the same crop on the same patch of ground twice in a row, and aims at ideally keeping a three-year gap. By rotating crops in this way, soil dwelling pests that take a particular fancy to any one type of veg are prevented from becoming established by moving their chosen food source elsewhere. Also, different veggies extract different nutrients and goodness from the earth. By continually changing the positions of his crops, Dirty Nails prevents the soil from becoming unbalanced or nutritionally

NATURAL HISTORY IN THE GARDEN
Robins

One of the most common birds to be heard in this part of winter is the red-breasted cock robin. He likes to sit high up in the branches of a tree and mark his territory with a song that is a thin, watery, sad but sweet warble.

depleted. As a rule, well manured ground that grows brassicas this year will be good for roots (including potatoes) next, followed by peas, beans, onions, salads or fruiting veg the year after that. Once again, pen and paper are extremely helpful as Dirty Nails literally maps out his crop plan.

VEGETABLE SNIPPETS
SOIL
HAND TEXTURE TEST

Most UK soils are what is known as mineral soils. They are formed by the gradual breaking down (erosion) of the underlying rocks (parent material) over geological time, which is measured over millions of years. Soil textures are known as sandy, silty or clayey, depending on the dominant particle size from which it comprises (in descending order, sand is the largest, then silt, then clay).

These classifications have important repercussions in the veg patch in terms of moisture and nutrient holding abilities. For example, a light, sandy soil is free-draining, whereas heavy clays are not. A lighter soil is liable to become impoverished more quickly than a heavy medium which can retain much of the essential goodness for longer. Those with a silty disposition are prone to erosion, especially when wet and on a slope.

Chalky soils occur over large areas of the UK. These tend to be thin and alkaline, demanding the addition of copious amounts of bulky farmyard manure and composts. Adequately tended, the pH balance is restored to more favourable conditions for a wider range of crops, and decent harvests of fruit, brassicas and legumes in particular are to be had. Loamy soils, where there is a more balanced mix of different sized particles, are considered to be ideal for veg cultivation. They warm up quickly in the spring, are comfortable to work, and retain both water and nutrients well without becoming saturated. Many crops prefer certain types of ground, and these factors all need to be considered when deciding what to plant and where.

Texture is easy to determine on the plot. A golf-ball sized ball of soil is gathered up and kneaded in the hands. Water can be added if needs be, so that it is uniformly moist, but not wet. When the ball has been massaged to an even consistency, it is ready to tell its tale.

By moulding it into balls, sausages and rings, the main texture groups can be determined as follows:

no ball = sand
crumbly ball = loamy sand
firm ball = sandy loam
crumbly sausage = silt loam
firm sausage = medium loam
forms a ring = clay loam
shiny ring = clay
shiny gritty ring = sandy clay.

PLANTING BUSH APPLES

January, 2nd Week

This is a good time of year to plant apple trees, as long as the weather is not too severe and the ground isn't waterlogged or frozen. Dirty Nails gets enormous pleasure from tending his collection of fruit trees.

Bush apples
Some of Dirty Nails' apples are grown as 'bush' trees, which are ideal where space is limited. With apples, the final size of the tree is dictated by what rootstock the variety is grafted onto. Bush apples can be grown on a number of different rootstock, but his are on what is called M26, which is relatively dwarfing. The full-grown tree should attain no more than roughly 10 feet (3 metres) in height, and the fruit will be within easy reach for harvesting. He has planted his bush apples with 12 feet (3.6 metres) spacings.

Dirty Nails grows varieties of apple that all come into blossom together. This is an important factor, as most apple trees will set a better crop if pollinated by another variety flowering at more or less the same time. Merton Knave, Worcester Permain, Sunset, Blenheim Orange, Pixie and Wagener are all dessert (or 'eating') apples. They should provide ripe fruit to munch on from late-August (Merton Knave, picked and eaten straight from the tree) through to March (Wagener, picked in October and stored carefully).

Dirty Nails buys his fruit trees as one-year old 'maiden whips', which means that they are a single stem (scion) grafted onto the rootstock. He is very fussy about where he sources his trees from. He only buys from a well-known West Country nursery that produces an excellent, informative catalogue, and where staff can answer all queries with authority over the phone. Delivery to the door is crucial too, because often there is no time for big trips out.

Planting
The maidens should arrive tied in bags, with straw or similar wrapped around the roots. They can be kept under cover like this for a while if planting conditions are unfavourable at that time. The sunny site will have been thoroughly cleared and weeded beforehand. Dirty Nails plants the apple trees with as little disturbance to the soil as possible. He levers a slot open with a spade and spreads the roots down into this gently with his fingers. If the soil is fairly good there is no need for fertilisers. Fresh manure is definitely a no-no because it will burn the root tips.

Great care must be taken

at this stage to ensure that the junction of scion and rootstock is kept well clear of the ground, and the soil mark on the stem coincides with the soil level after the slot has been firmly, but carefully, closed snugly around the roots with lightly stamping feet. Air pockets must also be avoided or else the roots, and therefore the tree, are liable to suffer.

No staking is needed for bush apples planted like this. Any natural movement of stem in the wind will only encourage strong root growth. All that remains, for now, is to apply a goodly bucket of water, one per tree, and to keep well moist throughout the first summer.

VEGETABLE SNIPPETS
APPLE ROOTSTOCKS EXPLAINED

Rootstocks are prefixed with 'M' or 'MM'. The former were developed at the East Malling Research Station in Kent, while the latter came to fruition at Merton Malling. Between them, they have revolutionised apple cultivation for the home producer. Trees can be nurtured on rootstock which is adapted to suit local conditions and available space, from good soil to poor, large acreages to backyards and pots.

• M27 is 'extremely dwarfing'. Fully cropping after five years, an apple tree on this rootstock will never grow taller than an average man. Trees should be staked for support, and surrounding soil should be well fed.

• M9 is 'very dwarfing', with maximum cropping potential realised a year or two later than those on M27. Ten feet (3 metres) is the usual full-grown height. They will need full-time supports and seasonal feeding. M9 is a good choice for apple trees in a small garden.

• M26 is 'dwarfing', and what Dirty Nails cultivates his bush apples on.

• MM106 is deemed 'semi-dwarfing' or 'semi vigorous', and used to grow half-standard trees. They reach maximum cropping potential after eight years, but will be producing fruits in half that time. Fully grown MM106 apple trees may be up to 20 feet (6 metres) in height, and are thus ideal for medium-sized gardens.

• MM111 (M25) is the rootstock of choice if a vigorous standard tree is desired. It is the perfect rootstock for large gardens or orchards. Within ten years a heavy crop will bear annually, but take care whilst picking - a ladder will be essential for reaching the uppermost boughs and branches.

CUPS OF TEA AND COBNUTS

Cups of tea

It has been a frustrating week for Dirty Nails. It does not happen very often, but from time to time the hectic work/family agenda means that there is not a lot of time to get outside and tend the land, beyond having a quick cup of tea and a look. Happily, by doing a little and often, he is pretty well on top of everything and there isn't much demanding immediate attention. Nevertheless Dirty Nails likes to get his hands in the soil as much as possible, and the weekend came as welcome respite from other commitments. A refreshing opportunity to harvest the week's veg and have a good scratch around. He is still trying to work out where to plant his crops for this coming season and is constantly changing his mind!

Cobnuts

Nothing stays still in the garden. Spring feels almost touchable on days when the wind drops and the sun shines. In the orchard Dirty Nails cultivates cobnuts and filberts. He has four varieties on the go: Nottingham Cob (Pearson's Prolific), Cosford Cob, Lambert's Filbert (Kent Cob), White Filbert. These are all domesticated varieties of the southern hazel, and sourced from a reliable nursery. Catkins, which are the male flower, festoon each bush, and those on the Nottingham Cob have already opened out. They resemble lambs' tails and in a breeze little clouds of pollen are released and carried in the air. The female flowers, which are minute red stars borne at the tips of fat buds, receive this pollen

NATURAL HISTORY IN THE GARDEN
Long-tailed Tits

Long-tailed tits are tiny black, grey and pink birds. In adults over half of their 5½ inch (14 cm) length is made up by their tails. Long-tailed tits always live in groups except during the breeding season, and there are often little flocks of them to be seen, flitting and dancing through the leafless canopy of trees growing just over the back of Dirty Nails' back garden wall. They search for spiders and insects hiding in amongst the branches, and are easily identified by their distinctive tail feathers and mischievous, twittering calls.

and the act of fertilisation occurs. Dirty Nails is hoping for a bumper crop of nuts this autumn.

Cobnuts and filberts can be planted at this time of year if bare-rooted, or any time if pot-grown. Either way, they should be cultivated with at least 3 feet (90 cm) all round. They prefer a deep, moist soil in sheltered areas and tolerate light shade. Dirty Nails has planted his to create a food-producing hedge.

VEGETABLE SNIPPETS
HERB TEAS AND CABBAGE WATER

Herbs from the garden are perfect for making a cup of refreshing, stimulating tea. At this time of year choice may not be so great, but if any young sprigs are available they can be popped into a mug and boiling water applied, no fuss, no bother. Alternatively a selection of leaves, dried in the summer, can be used. Fennel, lavender and mint are obvious candidates.

Truth is that Dirty Nails rarely, if ever, makes tea out of herbs growing in the garden. In the hot beverage department, he knows what he likes. Any traditional (organic) tea that is fair-traded is good by him, with a splash of this and a spoonful of that, for nursing and sipping whilst having a think and a look on a cold winter's day. Having said that, he is rather partial to a steaming hot mug of cabbage water, especially with a bit of vegetable stock stirred in to savoury it up a bit.

CHITTING POTATOES

Potatoes are a valuable and versatile vegetable. By growing different types of spud, Dirty Nails is able to keep his family well supplied with these tasty tubers for much of the year. He grows first early spuds, which offer 'new' potatoes fresh from the earth around midsummer, second earlies which are ready later in the season, and maincrop varieties which will store well for use throughout the winter. Growing a salad potato such as Pink Fir Apple is a good idea if ground is available. Cooked 'til tender, then tossed in an olive oil based dressing or similar, they add another dimension to potato consumption.

As well as different types of spud, there are also numerous varieties. They each possess their own particular strengths and qualities. It is well worth taking the time to find out what varieties are suited to the locality where they are to be planted. With this in mind, Dirty Nails prefers to select Concorde first early and Kestrel second early because they taste so wonderful, and succeed on his plot. He likes to experiment with maincrop varieties, reading the technical blurb to guide him and trying a new one each year.

Chitting

Dirty Nails won't be planting spuds until March, weather permitting, but work for this year's crop begins now. He has purchased his stock of certified disease-free seed potatoes this week. He likes to have them in hand early in the year and set them out for chitting. Each spud has a number of

NATURAL HISTORY IN THE GARDEN
Badgers in January

Look out for shallow holes and scratched up soil in and around the garden. These are 'snuffle holes' and are the work of badgers. These handsome black and white fellows, who have made a gentle living in our countryside for thousands of years, are pretty quiet and inactive at this time of year. However a mild spell will tempt them out of their underground home, or sett, to look for earthworms, their favourite food, and beetles.

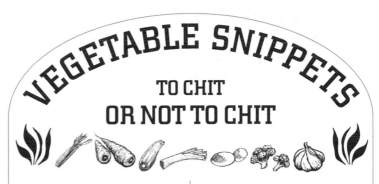

VEGETABLE SNIPPETS

TO CHIT OR NOT TO CHIT

'eyes' which are barely discernable now, but will soon produce shoots. These shoots, which should be dark and stout, are the chits.

For chitting Dirty Nails sets his spuds out in trays, touching and in a single layer, with eyes uppermost. He keeps them in a cool, light and frost-free place. The greenhouse is ideal. If severe weather threatens he will cover the trays with newspaper to protect them from any risk of frost. No water is needed, just a check over from time to time. If the shoots appear spindly and/or pale in colour, then more daylight is required. Spuds demand careful handling at all times, as they bruise easily. Chitting potatoes always gives Dirty Nails a little thrill, because it heralds the beginning of his annual spud growing rituals.

To chit, or not to chit, that is the question! Pre-sprouting spuds prior to planting has been part of the potato grower's list of essential jobs-to-do throughout the long and glorious history of this most versatile of vegetables, but need it be so? A qualified 'yes' is the answer, depending on what the home producer wants to dig up for dinner.

Fast-growing first and second early potatoes do crop earlier and heavier if chitted. With maincrops, which have a longer growing season before reaching maturity, chitting actually makes little difference to the final haul. However chitted maincrop tubers will come to maturation quicker. This is worth bearing in mind, and can be a useful tactic employed by the gardener in order to beat the disastrous and devastating blight. This is a fungal disease which is rife across the country and can strike in warm, humid weather anytime (usually from high-summer) when conditions are right.

Individual chits can be thinned out if desired, to three or four strong, good looking ones. Generally speaking, more chits equals more spuds, but smaller, whilst less chits translates to larger tatties, but less (ideal if a crop of decent sized bakers is required).

HEELING IN LEEKS AND NORTH FACING CHERRIES

Leeks

This week Dirty Nails has been heeling in leeks. Some of his fine crop of the Giant Winter variety are occupying ground that will soon be needed for other crops. With leeks, this is no problem. They are very hardy veg, easy to move and to store. He simply lifts the leeks that need shifting in the normal way and then transfers them to any handy area. Here he has already dug out a short trench 8 to 10 inches (20 to 25 cm) deep, and the leeks are placed into the trench close together. He packs soil all around the roots and shaft. Care is taken not to scatter crumbs down in between the leaf folds because this will make them gritty in the kitchen. Stored in this way, leeks will continue to stand in the ground happily for many weeks.

Cherries

Morello cherry thrives in the shade, and this tree is ideal for growing against a north-facing wall. It is a much sought after sour variety, ideal for culinary use. Dirty Nails prefers to leave his cherries unpicked for as long as he can get away with, and feast on the delicious fruits straight from the tree. He is training his morello cherry as a fan against the back of a shed. A two- or three-year old morello needs to be sourced from a reliable nursery, and planted during a mild spell any time between leaf-fall and bud-burst. This is roughly October until the end of February.

Planting is not complicated. Any fairly good soil is fine. A slot made with a spade, and levered open enough to receive the roots, is perfect. To get the correct planting depth, a piece of wood can be laid over the

NATURAL HISTORY IN THE GARDEN
Lesser Celandine

One of the first flowers to appear each year is the lesser celandine. Celandines grow thickly amongst banks and hedge-bottoms, and their yellow, buttercup-like flowers will be coming out in ever increasing numbers as the month passes.

In dull or wet weather the blooms close, but when the sun shines they open their little petals widely.

Celandine leaves are delicious when chopped finely with onions, parsley and herbs to make a salad dressing.

January, 5th Week

hole. By keeping the soil mark on the tree stem level with the wood, Dirty Nails ensures that he does not plant his tree either too deep or too shallow. The fibrous roots are pushed down into the crevice with his fingers, and soil is closed around them gently, but firmly, with the sole of his boot.

Regular watering during the first growing season is essential. Formative pruning at this stage involves selecting branches growing nearly opposite each other and snipping off the others with secateurs. The branches are then tied in to a network of canes, wired into position beforehand, to create a herring-bone effect. He leaves the leading shoot uncut for now.

Dirty Nails loves his morello cherry. Apart from thriving in a position where most plants would struggle, it is self-fertile. One tree should provide a bountiful crop for years to come.

VEGETABLE SNIPPETS
MORE LEEK FACTOIDS

Historically, it is said that Phoenician traders introduced leeks into Wales. According to legend it was 640 AD when King Cadwaller of the Britons found his men sorely pressed by invading Saxons. Cadwaller ordered the troops to wear leeks in their hats, to identify them and show whose side they were on. The Briton armies were ultimately victorious, and adopted the lucky-charm leek as an emblem of national pride.

Eating leeks would also have aided these men, especially in the winter. Calcium, iron and vitamin C are all present in this vegetable. The heart benefits too, via improved blood circulation.

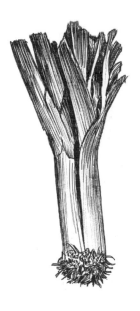

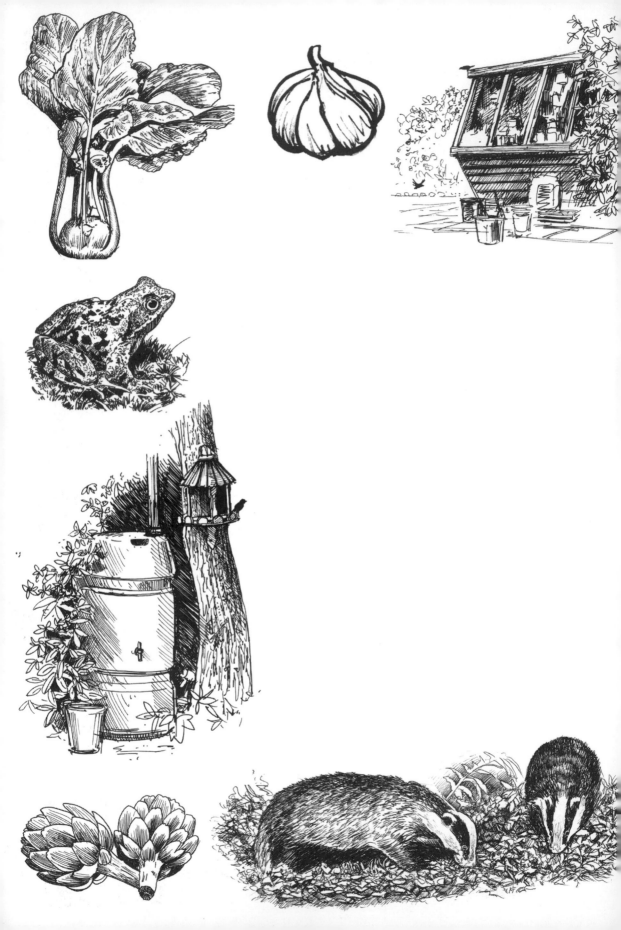

Jobs to do each week

JOBS TO DO EACH WEEK

In the Greenhouse

- Sow: autumn leeks, Carentan 2, in trays; wild rocket; Summer cabbage, Derby Day; strawberry, Temptation F1 and Alpine.

- Set up seed potatoes in trays to 'chit'.

On the Plot

- Potter and tidy.
- Secure horticultural fleece over globe artichoke crowns if frost threatens.
- Clean and turn neglected corners.
- Sprinkle lime on beds planned for brassicas.
- Sow: cauliflower, Snowball outdoors with protection.
- Tie-in fan-trained Morello cherry to herringbone network of canes.
- Tidy and sort out the shed.
- Construct permanent and semi-permanent paths in the veg patch.
- Make pigeon-scarers from old shredded plastic bags tied to canes, and secure netting over purple sprouting broccoli.

VEG ON THE MENU

FRESH
Salsify.
Leek.
Parsnip.
Celeriac.
Swede.
Scorzonera.
Kale.
Carrot.
Spring cabbage.
Purple sprouting.

FROM STORE
Spuds.
Beetroot.
Shallots.
Onions.
Garlic.

JOBS TO DO EACH WEEK

February, 2nd Week

In the Greenhouse

- Check seedlings.
- Sow: lettuces in trays, Trocadero and Buttercrunch; summer cabbage, Greyhound; radish in pots, Mixed Salad; globe artichoke, Green Globe.

On the Plot

- Potter and tidy.
- Hand-weed asparagus bed.
- Cut back hedges around the plot before the birds-nesting season.
- Hand-weed around globe artichoke crowns.
- Plant daffodil bulbs in and around fruit trees.
- Hand-weed around autumn-sown broad beans, rhubarb, horse-radish and winter onions.
- Keep clearing and turning beds over.

VEG ON THE MENU

FRESH
Perpetual spinach.
Jerusalem artichoke.
Celeriac.
Scorzonera.
Salsify.
Leek.
Spuds.
Kale.

FROM STORE
Onions.
Garlic.

JOBS TO DO EACH WEEK

In the Greenhouse

- Tend seedlings.
- Sow: turnip, White Globe and F1 Market Express.

On the Plot

- Prepare a sunny bed for cucumbers; erect chicken-wire against south-facing wall for them to scramble up and apply ample well-rotted manure to bed.
- Potter and tidy.
- Keep clearing and turning beds.
- Hand-weed around swedes.

VEG ON THE MENU

FRESH
Leek.
Parsnip.
Scorzonera.
Celearic.
Spring cabbage.
Jerusalem artichoke.
Leaf beet.

FROM STORE
Onions.
Garlic.
Squash.
Spuds.
Beetroot.

JOBS TO DO EACH WEEK

In the Greenhouse

• Tend seedlings.
• Keep on top of running repairs and maintenance jobs to gutters, seals, door hinges, glass etc..
• Purchase growing-bags and keep ready for later in the season.

On the Plot

• Make new paths with tree trunk rounds as 'stepping stones' in and around fruit trees.
• Keep harvesting Jerusalem artichokes, taking care to remove every last piece of tuber.
• Hand-weed here and there where crops have been harvested.
• Potter and tidy plot.
• Turn over cleaned soil.
• Plant broad beans, Witkiem, and protect with cloches.

VEG ON THE MENU

FRESH

Parsnip.
Swede.
Spring cabbage.
Leek.
Leaf beet.
Celeriac.
Salsify.

FROM STORE

Beetroot.
Spuds.
Squash.
Garlic.
Onions.

JOBS TO DO EACH WEEK

March, 1st Week

In the Greenhouse

- Check and tend seedlings.
- Sow: Brussels sprout, F1 Hybrid Millenium; cabbage, Derby Day; celeriac, Alablaster and Giant Prague; pepper, Ring o Fire, Long Red Marconi, Bendigo F1 (need heat, or remove to a sunny warm room in the house); Sugar Snap peas in pots; trays of leeks, Axima and Mammoth.

On the Plot

- Harvest the last Jerusalems, and top-dress site with compost to dig in later.
- Keep cleaning and turning areas as crops are harvested.
- Prepare a parsnip bed by turning and raking in a top-dressing of dry wood ash to a fine tilth.
- Sow parsnip seeds, White King, if not too cold.
- Turn and rake proposed onion bed. Rake and re-rake.
- Sow: radish, French breakfast (weather permitting).
- Broadcast-sow pot marigold seeds around plot edges.
- Plant-out over-wintered winter purslane with protection.
- Last chance to sensibly plant out bare-rooted trees on the plot or orchard. Some hazels are a good idea, including cultivated White Filberts.
- Scatter *Phacelia* seeds in plot corners for wildlife-rich green manure.
- Plant clumps of snowdrops 'in the green' in and around fruit trees.
- Mulch winter onions and over-wintered broad beans with compost.
- Spread manure over proposed potato patch.

VEG ON THE MENU

FRESH
Leek.
Scorzonera.
Swiss chard.
Winter purslane.
Parsnip.
Swede.
Celeriac.
Kale.
Spring cabbage.

FROM STORE
Onions.
Garlic.

JOBS TO DO EACH WEEK

March, 2nd Week

In the Greenhouse

- Check and tend seedlings.
- Sow: cabbage, Ormskirk Savoy and January King; lettuce, Talia; wild rocket; kohlrabi, Patrick F1; Swiss chard; leaf beet; nasturtiums in trays for planting out later.

On the Plot

- Sow: spring onion, Ishikura and Toga; radish, Sparkler; rainbow chard; carrot, Armetis F1.
- Deeply dig bed in preparation for sowing scorzonera.
- Continue to rake and re-rake onion bed prior to planting sets.
- Plant onions, Red Baron and Stuttgarter Giant.
- Prune-back White Filbert trees planted as bare rooters last week to half their size.
- Tidy, potter and prepare the plot.
- Dig trenches one spit deep for New Potatoes, and line with well-rotted manure.
- Harden-off Derby Day cabbages and turnips.

VEG ON THE MENU

FRESH
Leek.
Scorzonera.
Swiss chard.
Salsify.

FROM STORE
Onions.
Garlic.

JOBS TO DO EACH WEEK

In the Greenhouse

- Sow: tomatoes, Gardener's Delight and Britain's Breakfast; lettuce, Red Meveille; Brussels sprout, Wellington F1.
- Check and tend seedlings.

On the Plot

- Plant out First Early (Concorde) spuds.
- Check over onion sets and replant any dislodged by disturbance or pushed out by their own roots.
- Dig up any remaining leek plants from this season and heel-in to a bed close to the kitchen.
- Plant out Derby Day cabbages and protect with cloches.
- Remove bracken straw and twigs from around globe artichoke crowns (applied as winter protection).
- Dig out and store remaining scorzonera roots in boxes of dry compost.
- Prepare seed beds for direct sowing outdoors.
- Sow: carrot, Starca F1 and Flyaway F1 (weather permitting); parsnip, Avonresister (weather permitting).
- Plant out turnip seedlings, F1 Market Express and White Globe.
- Top-dress spuds with dry wood ash.

VEG ON THE MENU

FRESH
Parsnip.
Kale.
Leek.
Scorzonera.
Purple sprouting.
Spring cabbage.

FROM STORE
Onions.
Garlic.
Squash.

JOBS TO DO EACH WEEK

In the Greenhouse

- Sow: sunflower, Giant Single; cabbage, Derby Day; sugar Snap peas.
- Check and tend seedlings.

On the Plot

- Clear away the last parsnips and salsify; clamp in the garden close to the kitchen.
- Remove spent perpetual spinach plants to the compost heap.
- Dig trenches for Second Early and Maincrop potatoes.
- Sow: kohlrabi, Patrick F1; cauliflower, Snowball.
- Plant garlic cloves.
- Clear standing swedes and clamp with parsnips and salsify.
- Plant onion sets, Stuttgarter Giant, in prepared ground.
- Continue to check over onion sets and firm back any dislodged by weather, roots or birds.
- Sow: pot marigold around plot edges to deter invasive couch-grass.
- Put any spare grass clippings direct into spud trenches.
- Plant out lettuce (Buttercrunch) seedlings.
- Sow: beetroot, Detroit 2 and Mona Lisa.

VEG ON THE MENU

FRESH
Scorzonera.
Purple sprouting.
Parsnip.
Swede.
Leek.
Celeriac.

FROM STORE
Garlic.

JOBS TO DO EACH WEEK

In the Greenhouse

- Sow: aubergine, Long Tom.
- Check over seedlings.
- Keep up supplies of seed compost and peat-free multi-purpose compost for use as and when required.
- Pot-on wild rocket.
- Pot-on Sugar Snap peas.

On the Plot

- Hand-weed shallots planted on Winter Solstice and top-dress with dry wood ash.
- Check over all plots.
- Mulch garlic planted late-autumn with grass clippings.
- Clear and weed a bed for salsify, rake to a fine tilth and sow seeds.
- Prepare seed beds for leaf beet and carrots.
- Sow: carrots, Berlicum; and leaf beet.
- Keep outdoor sowings moist with a fine rose-ended watering can if rain is not forthcoming.
- Rake scorzonera bed to a fine tilth, then plant seeds.
- Clear and turn neglected parts of the plot not set aside for wildlife.
- Broadcast-sow wildflower seeds amongst fruit trees.
- Harden-off leeks, Carentan 2; and Derby Day cabbage.
- Gather supplies of bean-poles.
- Plant out Carentan 2 leeks into a nursery bed either this week or next.

VEG ON THE MENU

FRESH
Purple sprouting.
Parsnip.
Spring cabbage.
Leek.

FROM STORE
Onions.
Shallots.
Squash.
Garlic.

JOBS TO DO EACH WEEK

In the Greenhouse

- Sow: leek, Giant Winter, in trays; lettuce, Salad Bowl and Winter Density; squash, Butternut Waltham.
- Tend to the needs of seedlings.
- Pot-on sunflower, Giant Single, into larger containers.
- Pot-on Brussels sprouts, Hybrid Millenium.

On the Plot

- Trim grass around plot edges.
- Hand-weed asparagus bed.
- Put out lettuce, cabbage and rocket seedlings to harden off.
- Place cloches over Sugar Snap peas at night, remove daytime.
- Hand-weed autumn-sown Aquadulce broad beans.
- Plant out Talia lettuce seedlings under cloches.
- Check all areas and crops.
- Cut tops off remaining spring cabbages and cut cross slits on the stump end to encourage new growth.
- Cut anti-cabbage root fly collars from carpet underlay and store for use.
- Plant out cabbages, Derby Day.
- Rake level remaining rough-dug areas.
- Sow: turnip, White Globe; Wild rocket; spring onion, Ramrod; radish, Cherry Bell; beetroot, Detroit 2.
- Plant out young kohl-rabi, Patrick F1, plants.
- First thinning required for Armetis carrots sown early March.
- Plant Second Early (Kestrel) spuds.
- Hoe open ground if the soil surface is dry.

VEG ON THE MENU

FRESH
Winter purslane.
Corn salad.
Purple sprouting.
Lettuce.
Parsnip.
Leek.
Salsify.
Radish.

FROM STORE
Onions.
Garlic.

JOBS TO DO EACH WEEK

April, 2nd Week

In the Greenhouse

- Sow: Sugar Snap peas; cabbage, Greyhound; tomato, San Marzano and Gardeners Delight; sweetcorn, Mini-Pop; lettuce, Buttercrunch and Talia; dwarf French bean, Hildora; squash, Spaghetti, Sunburst F1 and Blue Ballet; courgette, Goldrush, Black Beauty, Dundoo F1; marrow, Long green Bush; cucumbers, Gherkin, Marketmore, King George.
- Prick-out Alpine strawberries into pots.
- Pot-on Wellington Brussels sprouts.
- Tend all seedlings and keep moist but not wet.

On the Plot

- Put citrus (lemon and lime) outside in the sunniest place possible.
- Keep all crops moist.
- Plant out lettuce All-Year-Round and Talia.
- Trim plot edges.

- Remove invading couch and other grasses from the comfrey patch.
- Erect wigwam of hazel twigs for peas in pots to climb up.
- Sow: carrots, Starca and Flyaway; turnip, F1 Market Express; radish, French Breakfast.
- Dig out any overlooked spuds from last year that are sprouting as weeds.
- Dig trench for Pink Fir Apple salad potatoes.
- Plant out rocket.
- Plant out lettuce, Red Merveille.
- Hoe winter onions.
- Hand-weed main crop onion sets recently planted.
- Stuff old wormery choc-full with nettles and comfrey after straining all remaining juice into bottles for liquid fertiliser and emptying old contents onto the plot as a mulch for fruit trees.
- Plant out cabbage, Derby Day.
- Dig out and compost spent spring cabbage unless harvesting new shoots.

VEG ON THE MENU

FRESH
Rocket.
Winter purslane.
Lettuce.
Radish.
Rhubarb.
Purple sprouting.

FROM STORE
None used

JOBS TO DO EACH WEEK

In the Greenhouse
- Plant runner beans, Liberty and Enorma. Dwarf French bean, Purple Teepee. Pea, Sugar Snap.
- Pot-on Alpine strawberries and Temptation F1 sown early-February.
- Start to pot-up tomato seedlings.
- Sow: aubergine, Long Tom; strawberry, Temptation F1.
- Keep all crops moist.

On the Plot
- Plant asparagus crowns.
- Plant out leaf beet and Swiss chard.
- Cut back encroaching brambles from blackcurrant and gooseberry bushes.
- Check all crops.
- Thin salsify seedlings.
- Keep on weeding.
- Potter about and enjoy this fantastic time of the year!

- Plant out cabbages, Greyhound.
- Thin scorzonera seedlings.
- Plant out Brussels sprouts, Millenium F1, into firm ground and fit with collars.
- Hoe if soil surface is dry.
- Dig up rogue spuds as they appear in unwanted places.
- Check over parsnips for signs of a fledgling crop amongst the weeds.
- Mulch onions with grass mowings.
- Sow: beetroot, Mona Lisa; spring onion; Ishikura; radish, Cherry Bell; carrot, Nantes 2.
- Plant out Sugar Snap peas sown end of March.
- Sow: land (American) cress; corn salad (Lambs Lettuce).

VEG ON THE MENU

FRESH
Winter purslane.
Lettuce.

FROM STORE
Onions.
Garlic.

JOBS TO DO EACH WEEK

In the Greenhouse

- Sow: cabbage, January King and Ormskirk Savoy; Brussels sprout, Hybrid Millenium F1.
- Pot-on tomatoes, Gardeners Delight, Britain's Breakfast.
- Tend all seedlings and crops.
- Plant runner beans, Liberty.

On the Plot

- Hand-weed asparagus bed.
- Slash back encroaching brambles.
- Hand-weed through winter onions.
- Water crops if needs be.
- Mulch autumn-sown Aquadulce broad beans with fresh grass mowings.
- Plant out winter cabbages, January King and Ormskirk Savoy sown earlier in the year. Fit with collars to dissuade the cabbage root fly.
- Weed amongst beetroot seedlings.

- String-up takeaway cartons on sticks to keep pigeons off brassicas.
- Re-sow parsnips, White King if germination has been patchy.
- Plant Maincrop spuds, Sante.
- Sow: dwarf French beans, Royalty; broad beans, Bunyards Exhibition.
- Weed amongst new shoots of Jerusalem artichoke.
- Take a delivery of straw for mulching marrows and squashes later in the summer.
- Check over all crops regularly.
- Finish planting out salad potatoes.
- Plant out leeks, Axima and Mammoth, into a nursery bed.
- Plant out sunflowers.
- Sow: lettuce, Trocadero, Buttercrunch, Talia; leaf beet; Florence fennel, Zefa Fino; beetroot, Boltardy and Detroit 2; turnip, White Globe; coriander, Leisure.

VEG ON THE MENU

FRESH
Winter purslane.
Lettuce.
Purple sprouting.
Radish.
Red lettuce.
Stinging nettle.

FROM STORE
Onions.
Garlic.

JOBS TO DO EACH WEEK

In the Greenhouse

- Sow: peas, Sugar Snap; purple sprouting, Late; cauliflower, Snow March; sweetcorn, Mini-Pop and Double Standard; dwarf French bean, Hildora and Purple Teepee.
- Pot-on tomato, Gardener's Delight.
- Tend all seedlings.
- Tidy and sort.
- Set up growbags on benches ready for greenhouse crops.
- Plant tomatoes and peppers into growbags.

On the Plot

- Liquid-feed citrus trees.
- Plant swedes in-between rows of ripening winter onions.
- Check over all crops.
- Earth-up First Early spuds.
- Sow: spring onion, Ramrod; carrot, Nantes 2; radish, French Breakfast 3.
- Keep on top of the weeding, especially horsetail and bindweed.
- Cut edges of plot to keep clear and tidy.
- Hand-weed amongst salsify.
- Tidy out the shed.
- Harden-off Sugar Snap peas.
- Plant out celeriac, Alablaster and Giant Prague.
- Clear away spent purple sprouting plants to the compost heap.
- Keep weeding asparagus bed. Do not cut any spears on crowns less than 2 years old.

VEG ON THE MENU

FRESH
Lettuce, Lobjoits Green Cos.
Winter purslane.
Radish, French Breakfast and Cherry Bell.
Winter onions.
Purple sprouting.

FROM STORE
Garlic.

JOBS TO DO EACH WEEK

In the Greenhouse
- Water and tend crops.
- Plant runner beans, White Emergo. Marrow, Long Green Bush.
- Put runners and curcubits outside for hardening-off.
- Keep water butts filled.

On the Plot
- Cut back and weed plot edges to keep on top of things.
- Keep paths clear.
- Hand-weed amongst seedling crops.
- Hand-weed asparagus.
- Cut no more than a couple of two-year old asparagus spears per plant.
- Hoe whenever you can.
- Plant-out nasturtiums in odd places.
- Earth-up Second Early spuds.
- Water seedlings if conditions are dry.
- Plant-out French and runner beans, Hildora, Liberty and Enorma.
- Earth-up First Early spuds.
- Plant-out lettuces, Salad Bowl, Buttercrunch and Talia.
- Liquid feed for broad beans, established lettuces, greens, spinach and chard.
- Weed peas.
- Plant-out courgettes, Goldrush, Black Beauty, Dundoo F1 and Sunburst.
- Tend tiny parsnips.
- Sow: carrot, Armetis F1; spring onion, Ishikura.
- Weed garlic patch.
- Prepare a seedbed for beetroot.

VEG ON THE MENU

FRESH
Lettuce.
Radish.
Winter onions.

FROM STORE
None used

JOBS TO DO EACH WEEK

In the Greenhouse
- Keep crops moist but not wet.
- Sow home-saved squash seeds from last year.
- More sorting to make room for tomatoes and sweetcorn in growbags.
- Pot-on aubergine, Long Tom.

On the Plot
- Thoroughly hand-weed through the parsnips.
- Water peas, beans and curcubits especially, and other crops if they are dry.
- Plant-out celeriac, Giant Prague; globe artichokes; leeks, Giant Winter, in nursery bed; lettuce, Salad Bowl; spaghetti squash.
- Cut back plot edges as and when…
- Tend nursery beds of leeks.
- Liquid feed for all established crops.
- Generous dose of water for fruit trees.
- Earth-up Second early spuds.
- Weed amongst scorzonera, salsify, Jerusalem artichokes and beets.
- Hoe at every opportunity.
- Hand-weed onions and shallots, globe artichokes, rhubarb and horseradish.
- Cut more nettles and comfrey for liquid-feed bin.

VEG ON THE MENU

FRESH
Turnip, White Globe.
Winter onions.
Lettuce.
Rocket.
Winter purslane.
Radish.
Globe artichoke.

FROM STORE
None used

JOBS TO DO EACH WEEK

May, 4th Week

In the Greenhouse
- Tend all crops.
- Into growbags, plant sweet corn (Double Standard, Mini-pop), cucumber (Gherkin, Marketmore, King George), tomato (Gardener's Delight).
- Water growbags daily.

On the Plot
- Water all crops with a watering can to get water where you want it – at the roots.
- Generous watering for asparagus bed.
- Keep paths clear and cut grass.
- Take delivery of sacks of horse manure for later use.
- Plant-out Sugar Snap peas in rows or in pots with support.
- Plant-out strawberries, Temptation F1; squash, Butternut Waltham; marrow, Long Green Bush; cauliflower, Snowball.
- Earth-up spuds.
- Hand-weed asparagus bed.
- Sow: lettuce, Sandringham, Iceberg; beetroot, Cylindra.
- Plant-out cabbages (January King), dwarf French bean (Hildora), Brussels sprout (F1 Hybrid Millenium), kale (Dwarf Green Curled).
- Tend crops.
- Tidy up broad beans.
- Weeding and thinning rows of seedlings.

VEG ON THE MENU

FRESH
Winter purslane.
Rocket.
Radish.
Lettuce.

FROM STORE
None used

JOBS TO DO EACH WEEK

May, 5th Week

In the Greenhouse
- Water all crops and seedlings, keeping moist but not wet.
- Veg in growbags need daily watering.

On the Plot
- Water crops as and when they look dry on top.
- Plant out Alpine strawberries in a shady bed (around a north-facing Morello cherry is ideal).
- Plant out purple sprouting Early and Late.
- Liquid seaweed feed for dwarf French beans, Hildora.
- Cut back vegetation on the paths.
- Hand-weed parsnips.
- Plant out kale, Thousandhead, and cabbages, January King.
- Thin beetroot seedlings.
- Keep hoiking out last year's spuds which are sprouting as weeds and could pass on disease.
- Earth-up salad potatoes.
- Prepare leek bed.
- Hoe between lines of veg at every opportunity.
- Plant out squash plants in a sunny bed.
- Keep an eye out for blackfly on broad beans. Spray with weak dilution of biodegradable washing-up liqiud or, preferably, pinch out tender growing tips.
- Earth-up Second Early and Maincrop spuds.
- Weed leek nursery bed.
- Take time to just stand and stare. This is a wonderful time of the year!

VEG ON THE MENU

FRESH
Radish, French Breakfast and Cherry Bell.
Winter onions.
Talia and Buttercrunch Lettuce,
Carrot, Starca F1.
Globe artichoke.
Broad beans, Aquadulce.
Swiss chard.
Perpetual spinach.

FROM STORE
None used

JOBS TO DO EACH WEEK

In the Greenhouse
- Daily watering for tomatoes, peppers, sweetcorn and other crops in growbags.
- Plant aubergine, Long Tom, in growbags.
- Tie supporting strings to roof girders for cucumbers to climb up.
- Pot-up okra, Pure Luck.

On the Plot
- Keep on watering direct by hand (to the base of crops and the roots) and hoeing.
- Finish preparing the main crop leek bed, clearing, digging and raking to a level.
- Import bags of manure and green waste from wherever possible for future use.
- Tend veggies and look over daily.
- Plant out kale, Westland Winter; cabbage, Ormskirk Savoy.

- Drench spuds with a hose if no rain is in the area.
- Plant out runner beans, White Emergo; tomatoes, San Marzano and Gardener's Delight, in sunniest bed possible.
- Water all fruit trees with at least two good bucket-loads. Pour it around the roots slowly so water has a chance to get into the ground and not run off.
- Thin lettuces, Talia.
- Plant out Axima leeks and puddle-in.
- Harvest winter (Radar) onions.
- Earth-up Maincrop and Salad potatoes.

VEG ON THE MENU

FRESH
Broad beans, Aquadulce.
Winter onions.
Radish, Cherry Bell and French Breakfast.
Lettuce, Buttercrunch and Talia.
Sugar Snap peas.
Turnip, White Globe.
Rocket.
Globe artichoke.
Perpetual spinach.
Swiss chard.
Carrot.
Shallots.

FROM STORE
None used

JOBS TO DO EACH WEEK

June, 2nd Week

In the Greenhouse

- Keep all crops moist but not wet by watering daily.
- Put supports for tomatoes in place.

On the Plot

- Puddle-in Axima leeks daily all week if possible.
- Keep crops watered direct to the roots if rain is not forthcoming.
- Plant out squashes and marrows, and give a good dose of water.
- Harvest shallots sown on the Winter Solstice when the tops have died down and conditions are dry.
- Hand-weed around purple sprouting and kale.
- Hoe between rows of parsnips, then hand-weed between the plants.
- Hoe swede bed.
- Hand-weed Giant Winter leek nursery bed, and prepare a bed for planting-out soon.
- Keep brassicas well watered.
- Tie sunflowers to supporting poles.
- Sow: radish, French Breakfast; kohlrabi, Delikatess.

VEG ON THE MENU

FRESH
Broad beans.
Winter onions.
Lettuce, Talia and All-Year-Round.
Rocket.
Sugar Snap peas.
Globe artichoke.
Beetroot, Mona Lisa.
Lettuce, Red Merveille.
Spuds, Concorde.
Cabbage, Derby Day.
Carrot, Starca F1.

FROM STORE
None used

JOBS TO DO EACH WEEK

In the Greenhouse

- Tending and watering daily.
- Keep an eye out for pests and diseases.

On the Plot

- Earth-up Pink Fir Apple salad and Cara Maincrop spuds.
- Hand-weed asparagus bed.
- Tend purple sprouting.
- Gather harvested winter Radar onions, tie into bunches and hang up in a dry, airy place as cool as possible.
- Support broad beans with canes and string.
- Stake Brussels sprout plants, especially if there is a threat of summer storms.
- Put support system in for asparagus tops which are liable to blow in the wind and could damage the crowns at ground level. Stout posts at either end of the rows with string

tied tight in between should do the trick.
- Sow beetroot, Cylindra and Detroit 2.
- Hoe whenever the soil surface is dry.
- Hand-weed around Dwarf Green Curled kale.
- Cut tops off Jerusalem artichokes by half.
- Test ripeness of Witkiem broad beans by squeezing the plump pods to feel for bean development within.
- Mulch around courgettes and squashes with straw (will keep crop clean too).
- Keep bird scaring devices in good working order, especially around the cabbage patch.

VEG ON THE MENU

FRESH

Spuds, Concorde.
Cabbage, Derby Day.
Broad beans, Aquadulce.
Turnip, F1 Market Express.
Winter onions.
Lettuce, Red Merveille, All-Year-Round, Salad Bowl, Buttercrunch.
Rocket.
Spring onion, Toga.
Kohlrabi, Patrick.
Perpetual spinach.
Rainbow chard.
Swiss chard.
Sugar Snap peas.

FROM STORE

None used

JOBS TO DO EACH WEEK

In the Greenhouse

- Tend all crops.
- Cut lower leaves from tomatoes and pinch out shoots between leaf and stem (side shoots).
- Water crops daily to keep moist but not wet.

On the Plot

- Plant out Giant Winter leeks into prepared ground and puddle-in daily all week.
- Water squashes generously.
- Clear spent broad beans by cutting at ground level. Leave roots in the soil to slow-release nitrogen from the root nodules.
- Thin swedes to 9 or 10 inch (about 25cm) spacings.
- Tie string criss-crossed over swedes to deter pigeons.
- Make a fuss of the cat if rabbits are nibbling brassicas to encourage her to keep guard!
- Liquid feed for courgettes.
- Plant out Mammoth leeks into prepared bed.
- Keep all crops moist but not wet with targeted watering to the roots.
- Thin Boltardy and Cylindra beetroot.
- Plant out dwarf French beans, Tendergreen.
- Dig over patch where Derby Day cabbages were.
- Cut back Rainbow chard going to seed to encourage a new flush of growth, and pull out seeded spinach plants.
- Sow beetroot, Detroit 2.
- Compost spent Sugar Snap peas.
- Plant out White Sprouting plants.

VEG ON THE MENU

FRESH

Cabbage, Derby Day.
Carrot, Armetis.
Spring onions.
Turnip, F1 Market Express.
Rainbow chard.
Beetroot, Mona Lisa.
Perpetual spinach.
Rocket.
Broad beans, Witkiem.
Baby leeks, Carentan 2.
Dwarf Fench bean, Hildora.
Long Green Marrow (taken young).
Kohlrabi, Partick.
Courgette, Gold Rush.
Beetroot, Detroit 2.
Winter onions.
Spuds, Concorde.
Radar Onion.
Sugar snap peas.
Lettuce, Salad Bowl, Sandringham, Talia.
Corn salad.
Land cress.
Globe artichoke.

JOBS TO DO EACH WEEK

July, 1st Week

In the Greenhouse

- Water and liquid comfrey & nettle feed for crops beginning to fruit.
- Careful monitoring of plants, removing unhealthy foliage and keeping environment well ventilated.

On the Plot

- Hand-weed amongst purple sprouting and kale.
- Hoe through rows of leeks, and anywhere else regardless of whether weeds are visible or not.
- Hand-weed garlic before harvesting.
- Continue to puddle-in leeks whenever time permits.
- Keep globe artichokes well supplied with water.
- Spread garlic out in the sun to fully ripen.
- Cut back comfrey and remove to the liquid manure bin.

- Maintain tidy plot edges by cutting back all round.
- Liquid feed for all beans.
- Sow cabbage, Red Drumhead and Pixie, in pots and keep in partial shade.
- Tie-in tomato San Marzano, growing outdoors in containers, to supporting canes.
- Remove and burn any brassicas showing signs of disease.
- Plant dwarf French beans, Royalty.
- Sow carrots, Autumn King.
- Hand-weed asparagus bed.

VEG ON THE MENU

FRESH

Lettuce, All-Year-Round, Talia, Salad Bowl, Buttercrunch, Iceberg.
Rocket.
Winter onions.
Cabbage, Derby Day.
Land cress.
Turnip, F1Market Express.
Corn salad.
Spring onions.
Carrot, Armetis.
Broad beans, Witkiem.
Spuds, Concorde.
Kohlrabi.
Beetroot, Mona Lisa and Detroit 2.
Dwarf French bean, Hildora and Purple Teepee.
Red onions.
Cucumber, Gherkin.
Sugar Snap peas.
Courgette, Black Beauty and Goldrush.
Swiss chard.
Baby leek.

JOBS TO DO EACH WEEK

July, 2nd Week

In the Greenhouse

- Water all crops daily.
- Liquid feed.

On the Plot

- Thin latest beetroot sowings.
- Compost spent Sugar Snap peas in pots.
- Sow lines of lettuce, Enya and Montel.
- Hand-weed asparagus bed.
- Keep crops moist but not wet.
- Close weeding in amongst runner beans and lettuces.
- Clear exhausted Swiss chard.
- Apply mulch of well-rotted manure over bed where broad beans were (in preparation for cabbages).
- Get busy with the hoe whenever possible.
- Weed and clip plot edges.
- 'Summer prune' top-fruit trees.

- Sow: leaf beet and Swiss chard for winter and spring greens; spring onion, Guardsman; kohl-rabi, Delikatess; beetroot, Cylindra; turnip, Purple Top Milan.
- All crops in containers need plenty of good water.
- Clear and weed around globe artichoke crowns.
- Start regular inspections of brassicas for cabbage white butterfly eggs, and rub out with thumb where found.

VEG ON THE MENU

FRESH

Spuds, Concorde.
Globe artichoke.
Swiss chard.
Broad beans, Witkiem.
Lettuce, Talia, Salad Bowl, Iceberg, Buttercrunch.
Cucumber, Gherkin.
Dwarf French bean, Hildora and Purple Teepee.
Rainbow chard.
Sugar Snap peas.
Beetroot, Detriot 2.
Winter (Radar) onions.
Cabbage, Greyhound.
Radish, French Breakfast.
Land cress.
Corn salad.
Rocket.

JOBS TO DO EACH WEEK

July, 3rd Week

In the Greenhouse
- Water daily.
- Liquid feed once a week..
- Inspect all crops for pests and diseases.

On the Plot
- Keep up the watering direct to plant roots, especially curcubits, beans, globe artichokes, asparagus and rhubarb.
- Sow spring onions, White Lisbon Winter Hardy.
- Collect grass mowings wherever possible and add to the compost or mulch around crops (avoid any which have been chemically treated).
- Keep recent sowings moist.
- Take badger precautions if they are in your area at night by spraying urine around their favourite crops (spuds, parsnips, carrots).
- Hoe a little and often.
- Keep edges cut back and weeded.

- Give fruit trees a generous amount of water.
- Tie sunflowers to supporting canes or posts.
- Sow leaf beet.
- Cut down haulms of spuds showing any signs of blight and burn immediately.
- Clear Salad Bowl lettuces going to seed.

VEG ON THE MENU

FRESH
Beetroot, Mona Lisa.
Spuds, Concorde.
Cucumber, Marketmore.
Lettuce, Buttercrunch, Talia.
Radish, French Breakfast.
Spring onions.
Runner beans, Enorma.
Morello cherry.
Carrot.
Baby leek.
Marrow.
Courgette, Goldrush and Black Beauty.
Red onions.
Winter onions.
Shallots.
Garlic.
Globe artichoke.
Dwarf French beans, Hildora.
Beetroot, Detriot 2.

JOBS TO DO EACH WEEK

In the Greenhouse
- Water all crops daily.
- Feed tomatoes and aubergines once this week.
- Ensure adequate ventilation in hot weather.

On the Plot
- Weed and hoe here and there every time you pop up to the garden.
- Burn potato haulms that are blighted immediately.
- Hand-weed asparagus bed.
- Water late sowings of broad beans.
- Check Second Early and Maincrop spuds for any signs of blight.
- Water swedes.
- Badgers are very active this month. Protect root veg nightly by spraying with human urine.
- Give squashes, courgettes and marrows plenty to drink applied down at the roots.
- Same with all the brassicas and beans.
- Weed around globe artichoke crowns.
- Keep recently sown seeds moist in the hot sun. Water with a rose on the can either in the morning first thing or at night-time.
- Cut spud haulms if blight is spotted.

VEG ON THE MENU

FRESH
Spuds, Concorde.
Courgette, Black Beauty.
Leek, Carentan 2.
Carrot.
Runner beans.
Lettuce, Talia, Sandringham, Buttercrunch.
Cucumber, Marketmore, Gherkin.
Spring onion.
French beans, Purple Teepee, Hildora.
Radish, French Breakfast.
Swiss chard.
Beetroot.
Globe artichoke.
Red onions, Red Baron.
Squash, Sunburst.

FROM STORE
Garlic.
Winter 'Radar' onions.

JOBS TO DO EACH WEEK

In the Greenhouse

- Fertilise sweetcorn when flowers and tassels are showing by tapping the plants to release the pollen. Do this job daily, morning and night.
- Water all crops daily.
- Once-weekly liquid feed.

On the Plot

- Cut a third off the tops of Jerusalem artichokes to prevent wind damage.
- Remove dying foliage on globe artichokes to encourage new growth.
- Water all squashes, courgettes and marrows.
- Keep seedlings moist, but avoid watering in the hot daytime to avoid scorching tender foliage.
- Tie outdoor plum tomatoes to supporting canes, and water daily.
- Inspect the plot for badger damage.
- Hand-weed a little and often.

- Sow lettuce, Montel and Enya.
- Water beans and brassicas.
- Carefully hoe along lines of leeks, then hand-weed between the plants.
- Keep a check on ripening tomatoes! Cut off some leaves low down to allow the sunshine onto the fruit.
- Take nightly badger precautions.
- Check over all crops and water where needed.
- Pinch out rampant squash shoots to contain the bushy growth if it is smothering other veggies.
- Harvest onions if the weather is fine now but the August forecast is dodgy. Lift, tie in to bunches, and hang in a sheltered but airy place to dry. If the month is set fair onions can be left standing until early-September if needs be.

VEG ON THE MENU

FRESH
Spuds, Concorde.
Runner beans.
Carrot.
Onions, Red Baron.
Beetroot, Mona Lisa.
Marrow.
Cucumber, Gherkin and Marketmore.
Courgette.
Globe artichoke.

FROM STORE
Winter onions.
Garlic.

JOBS TO DO EACH WEEK

In the Greenhouse
- Check all crops for pests and diseases.
- Water all crops daily, and feed at end of the week.
- Jog sweetcorn when tassels are showing and in flower to release the pollen and ensure fertilisation. Do this morning and night every day.

On the Plot
- Hoe and weed whenever possible wherever unwanted growth is showing.
- Keep a sharp eye on Second Early and Maincrop spuds for signs of blight.
- Cut down and burn haulms if necessary.
- Badger precautions each evening.
- Plant out Red Drumhead cabbages into enriched, prepared ground.
- Plant out Pixie cabbages.

- Secure horticultural fleece over cabbages to keep off butterflies.
- Remove small globe artichoke heads that won't be useable but will sap energy from the plant.
- Water as and when desired.
- Start to clean weeds from potato patch, and commence harvesting of Second Earlies. Wash carefully and allow to fully dry in the sun before putting into store.
- Keep up watering outdoor tomatoes.

VEG ON THE MENU

FRESH
Runner beans.
Spuds, Concorde.
Carrot.
Globe artichoke.
Cucumber, Gherkin.
Tomato.
Broad beans.
Dwarf French beans.
Beetroot.
Red onions.
Courgette, Black Beauty.
Swiss chard.
Aubergine.
Baby leek.

FROM STORE
Winter 'Radar' onions.
Garlic.

JOBS TO DO EACH WEEK

In the Greenhouse

- Water crops daily.
- Pick tomatoes as they come into ripeness.
- Continue to simulate the wind by hand-fertilising sweetcorn if still in tassel and flower.

On the Plot

- Dig, clean, dry and store Second Early potatoes.
- Water all crops in containers daily.
- Hoe and weed as desired.
- Continue to weed the rows of cut-down spuds before harvesting.
- Remove tatty lower leaves on celeriac.
- Tidy and potter round the plot to keep everything shipshape.
- Cut down Swiss chard and leaf beet going to seed.
- Thin lettuce seedlings, and use thinnings either to plant elsewhere or enjoy as baby leaf salad.
- Keep the hoe busy in the mornings.
- Clear away pea sticks no longer in use.

VEG ON THE MENU

FRESH

Runner beans.
Spuds, Concorde and Kestrel.
Tomatoes.
Lettuce, Sandringham.
Cucumber.
Broad beans.
Onions.
Spring onions.
Aubergine.
Sweet peppers.
Courgette.
Red onions.
Perpetual spinach.
Florence fennel, Zefa Fino.
Rainbow chard.
Carrot.

FROM STORE

Garlic.
Winter 'Radar' onions.

JOBS TO DO EACH WEEK

In the Greenhouse

- Keep providing adequate ventilation in hot weather.
- Water daily.
- Liquid feed twice this week for veggies producing a crop.

On the Plot

- Tidy the shed in preparation for veg as produce comes in to store.
- Hang dried and bunched main crop onions in a cool, airy shed.
- Commence to dig main crop potatoes (can be delayed as late as end of September if there is no blight and top growth is looking healthy).
- Allow spuds to dry in the sun for a day after washing.
- Hand-weed asparagus bed.
- Burn any diseased tomato plants immediately.
- Cut nettles around compost heaps to allow easy access.
- Trim plot edges to maintain a tidy work space.
- Weed and hoe around leeks, brassicas and parsnips.
- Clean rows of Cylindra beetroot.
- Collect seeds of favourite flowers such as pot marigold, corn cockle, black knapweed, foxglove and great mullien in paper bags under dry conditions.
- Remove tiny globe artichoke heads which won't be eaten.
- Cut off any flowers shooting from salsify and scorzonera plants.
- Start to dig salad potatoes, Pink Fir Apples.

VEG ON THE MENU

FRESH

Outdoor tomatoes.
Spuds, Concorde, Kestrel and Cara.
Broad beans.
Courgette.
Cucumber.
Florence fennel, Zefa Fino.
Sweet peppers.
Aubergine.
Marrow.
Runner beans.
Red onions.
Land cress.
Beetroot.
Perpetual spinach (leaf beet).

FROM STORE

Winter onions.
Garlic.

JOBS TO DO EACH WEEK

August, 5th Week

In the Greenhouse
- Water crops daily.
- Twice weekly liquid feed for all.
- Remove leaves from tomatoes that are shading fruits.
- Keep an eye for pests and disease, react accordingly.

On the Plot
- Dig, wash, dry and store the last Maincrop spuds.
- Remove haulms, weed completely, and continue to do likewise with salad potatoes.
- Burn those haulms.
- Prune Morello cherry.
- Tie-in branches of 'step-over' apples to training wire.
- Hoe in amongst leeks.
- Water tomatoes in containers.
- Sling some well-rotted manure onto bed where First Early spuds were, fork in and rake to a level.
- Prepare a bed for winter 'Radar' onion sets by applying wood ash, raking to a crumbly tilth, treading firm with the 'gardeners shuffle', and repeating the process.
- Water and weed where needed (especially runner beans).
- Hoe open soil to keep weeds under control, then broadcast-sow a green manure if not needed for a few months.
- Give citrus trees in pots a fillip with some Epsom salts.
- Remove scale bugs from citrus by hand (look under the leaves).
- Tend strawberries.
- Weed amongst purple sprouting broccoli.

VEG ON THE MENU

FRESH
Squash, Sunburst.
Florence fennel.
Aubergine.
Marrow.
Green peppers.
Leaf beet.
Sweet pepper.
Beetroot.
Strawberry.
Courgette.
Carrot.
Broad beans.
Runner beans.
Tomatoes.
Leek, Carentan 2.
Cucumber.
Spring onions.
Rocket.
Lettuce.
Pink Fir Apple potato.
Globe artichoke.

FROM STORE
Red onions.
Garlic.
Spuds, Kestrel and Cara.

JOBS TO DO EACH WEEK

September, 1st Week

In the Greenhouse

- Carefully clear spent cucumbers and any other plants showing signs of disease such as grey mould (botrytis).
- Water peppers and aubergines daily.
- Ensure adequate ventilation.
- Water tomatoes every two or three days.
- Empty spent growbags onto the garden.
- Sow a tray of winter purslane (miner's lettuce).

On the Plot

- Plant winter 'Radar' onion sets.
- Continue to dig and prepare Pink Fir Apple spuds for storing.
- Plenty of water to the roots of squashes.
- Liquid-feed celeriac.
- Remove tatty celeriac lower leaves.
- Remove all grass mowings to the compost heap.
- Water all crops, especially brassicas.
- Continue to collect flowers seeds in fine dry weather for sowing next year.
- Clear encroaching vegetation from around fruit trees carefully with a hand-fork, water generously and mulch with bark chippings or well-rotted manure.
- Keep taking off leaves from outdoor tomatoes to hasten ripening.
- Check brassicas every other night for butterfly eggs and caterpillars. Crush the eggs and remove caterpillars to a sacrificial bed of nasturtiums elsewhere.
- Deposit manure and leaf mould onto the plot in piles ready for spreading.
- Clear spent rocket to the compost heap.
- Do the same with tired bean plants.

VEG ON THE MENU

FRESH
Strawberry.
Spring onions.
Tomatoes.
Sweet peppers.
Sweetcorn.
Carrot.
Beetroot.
Land cress.
Nasturtium.
Lettuce, Montel.
Chilli peppers.
Rocket.
Runner beans.
Leek, Carentan 2.
Florence fennel.
Aubergine.

FROM STORE
Winter onions.
Spuds.
Garlic.

JOBS TO DO EACH WEEK

In the Greenhouse

- Keep watering tomatoes, peppers, aubergines and other crops sparingly.
- Ensure newly sown seeds are kept moist.
- Sow lettuce, Winter Density and All-Year-Round.
- Remove plants as they are spent and burn (don't compost).

On the Plot

- Check everything.
- Put up shredded plastic bags on sticks to deter pigeons around brassicas including swedes.
- Collect and deliver tree leaves from wherever they can easily be gathered and deposit into a leaf mould bin.
- Keep the hoe busy between standing crops.
- Hand-weed asparagus.
- Keep harvesting courgettes and marrows.
- Cut back plot edges and paths.
- Mulch kale plants with mature manure.
- Check brassicas for caterpillars and eggs.
- Tie purple sprouting broccoli and kale to stakes to prevent wind damage this coming winter.
- Cut back encroaching brambles.
- Thoroughly clean soil where crops have been harvested and sow with green manure such as *phacelia* if not needed in the immediate future.
- Keep harvesting Pink Fir Apple spuds.
- Harvest the last globe artichoke if you are lucky!
- Harvest spaghetti squash crop.
- Hang main-crop onion haul in the shed.

VEG ON THE MENU

FRESH

Strawberry.
Runner beans.
Tomatoes.
Aubergine.
Sweet peppers.
Swiss chard.
Leek, Carentan 2.
Beetroot.
Courgette, Black beauty and Goldrush.
Lettuce.
Spring onions.
Carrot.
Cabbage, Greyhound.

FROM STORE

Spuds, Kestrel.
Onions.
Shallots.
Garlic.

JOBS TO DO EACH WEEK

In the Greenhouse

- Water crops every three days.
- Clear spent plants and growing medium.

On the Plot

- Lift fleece from Red Drumhead and Pixie cabbages to facilitate weeding, then replace.
- Empty contents of compost bin strategically in places on the plot.
- Hand-weed here and there as required.
- Keep collecting leaves and grass mowings.
- Hoe through parsnips, leeks and recently planted winter onion sets.
- Clear squash plants as they are harvested.
- Clear outdoor tomato plants.
- Strip off tough outside leaves from Swiss chard and perpetual spinach to encourage fresh growth.
- Sow corn salad.
- Maintain order in the shed.
- Regularly sniff stored veg (especially potatoes) and check for rotting articles.

VEG ON THE MENU

FRESH

Strawberry.
Tomatoes.
Aubergine.
Okra.
Sweet red and green peppers.
Courgette, Goldrush.
Florence fennel.
Sunburst squash.
Carrot.
Leaf beet.
Grape.
Beetroot.
Cucumber.
Nottingham cobnut.
Swiss chard.

FROM STORE

Onions.
Garlic.
Red onions.
Spuds.

153

JOBS TO DO EACH WEEK

In the Greenhouse
- Keep seedlings moist.
- Clear sweetcorn plants to the compost heap and put growbag contents on the garden.
- Remove and burn spent tomato and pepper plants.
- Keep watering aubergines, cucumbers, peppers and chillies every other day if still producing a harvest.

On the Plot
- Check potatoes in store, remove any bad ones.
- Continue to apply as much manure, molehills, leaf mould and compost to the plot as can be spared.
- Potter about and enjoy the mellowness of autumn.
- Turn over ground where squashes were after weeding thoroughly.
- Weed plot edges, especially removing the invasive white wiry threads of couch grass.
- Hand-weed winter onions.
- Hoe leeks.
- Cut back flower stalks on globe artichokes and remove tatty foliage.
- Compost dead and dying rhubarb stalks.
- Turn over a plot in preparation for winter salads and lettuces.
- Tidy away odds and ends.
- Sow green manure on ground to be left uncultivated over winter.

VEG ON THE MENU

FRESH
Courgette, Black Beauty and Goldrush.
Onion.
Sweet peppers.
Carrot.
Beetroot.
Lettuce.
Leek, Axima.
Turnip, Purple Top Milan.

FROM STORE
Red onions.
Garlic.
Shallots.
Spuds, Kestrel.

JOBS TO DO EACH WEEK

October, 1st Week

In the Greenhouse

- Continue to clear crops as plants become exhausted.
- Clean the gutters of fallen leaves.
- Harvest Ring o Fire chillis, and remove spent plants.
- Tidy pots, bags and accumulated rubbish.
- End of the week: remove entire contents onto wooden pallets to keep them clean, then clean the windows and sweep the floor. Wash the insides with biodegradable detergent thoroughly.

On the Plot

- Keep on collecting leaves from elsewhere and depositing in a suitable pile in the garden.
- Tidy round purple sprouting broccoli and kale by removing dead and dying lower leaves and weeding in the vicinity.
- Stake brassicas and earth-up the roots with topsoil or compost.
- Cut plot edges.
- Plant out winter purslane and Winter Density lettuce.
- Harvest butternut squashes.
- Clear hard-working courgette plants to refuse heap.
- Tie Brussels sprout plants to supporting canes.
- Plant out All-Year-Round lettuces.

VEG ON THE MENU

FRESH
Carrot.
Spring onions.
Lettuce.
Beetroot.
Celeriac, Giant Prague.
Cucumber.
Sweet peppers.
Tomatoes.
Swiss chard.
Leek.

FROM STORE
Red onions.
Spuds, Kestrel.
Sunburst squash.
Garlic.
Onions.

JOBS TO DO EACH WEEK

In the Greenhouse

- Carry out essential maintenance and repairs while it is empty.

On the Plot

- Check over all crops.
- Keep cleaning and turning vacant ground.
- Ensure that bird-scarers around the cabbage patch are in good order.
- Keep collecting leaves.
- Cover newly planted-out winter purslane with jam jars for protection.
- Sow broad beans, Imperial Green Windsor and Aquadulce.
- Feast your eyes on parsnips and swedes ready for harvest!

VEG ON THE MENU

FRESH

Celeriac.
Globe artichoke.
Courgette, Black Beauty.
Tomatoes.
Aubergine.
Beetroot, Cylindra.
Leek, Axima.
Swiss chard.
Turnip, Purple Top Milan.
Carrot.
Parsnip.
Swede, Marian.

FROM STORE

Butternut squash.
Red onions.
Spuds, Kestrel and Cara.
Garlic.
Onions.
Shallots.
Chilli pepper.

JOBS TO DO EACH WEEK

October, 3rd Week

In the Greenhouse

- Start to replace shelves and pots as they get washed.
- Pot-up strawberry plants.
- Pot-on All-Year-Round lettuces and winter purslane.
- Sow black knapweed seeds.
- Bring citrus trees in for over-winter protection.

On the Plot

- Tend parsnips by removing dead leaves and keeping the crowns tidy.
- Check over all crops.
- Stop scorzonera from flowering.
- Gather and store as many leaves as possible.
- Wash greenhouse contents at every opportunity, allow to dry and replace.
- Compost White Emergo runner bean plants.

VEG ON THE MENU

FRESH
Swede.
Carrot.
Parsnip.
Celeriac.
Lettuce.

FROM STORE
Garlic.
Red onions.
Spuds, Kestrel and Pink Fir Apple.
Chilli peppers.
Onions.
Shallots.
Spaghetti squash.

JOBS TO DO EACH WEEK

In the Greenhouse

- Tend to plants and seedlings.

On the Plot

- Put leaves on the leaf mould pile.
- Collect and store horse manure in bags.
- Cut down asparagus ferns.
- Weed asparagus bed.
- Stake and tie white sprouting broccoli.
- Wash greenhouse contents as and when.
- Tie-in branches on Morello cherry.
- Light pruning of pears.
- Plant garlic, Germidour.

VEG ON THE MENU

FRESH

Beetroot, Cylindra.
Swiss chard.
Leaf beet.
Leek, Axima.
Carrot.
Coriander.
Salsify.
Turnip, Purple Top Milan.
Celeriac.

FROM STORE

Spuds, Cara and Pink Fir Apple.
Onions.
Garlic.

JOBS TO DO EACH WEEK

In the Greenhouse

- Finish off essential maintenance jobs.
- Replace washed and disinfected pots, shelves and accessories.

On the Plot

- Cut down Jerusalem artichoke tops to just above ground level.
- Snip round plot edges to keep neat and tidy.
- Thoroughly weed asparagus bed and mulch with leaf mould or well-rotted manure.
- Tend winter onions with hand-weeding.
- Plant more garlic cloves.
- Dig over bed where courgettes were.
- Cut back and compost comfrey.
- Rake level leaf mould and compost on the plot.
- Hand-weed amongst the scorzonera.
- Use a garden fork to weed close to the edges and remove couch-grass.
- Tickle around amongst white sprouting broccoli and Brussels sprouts.
- Tear off withered lower leaves from celeriac.

VEG ON THE MENU

FRESH
Beetroot.
Jerusalem artichoke.
Leaf beet.
Lettuce.
Spring onions.
Carrot.
Leek, Axima.
Swede.
Parsnip.
Brussels sprouts.
Bramley apple.

FROM STORE
Spuds, Kestrel.
Red onions.
Squash.
Butternut squash.
Garlic.
Onions.

JOBS TO DO EACH WEEK

In the Greenhouse
- Check on plants.
- Water strawberries and winter purslane.

On the Plot
- Check all crops.
- Bring leaves onto the plot and store in a pile.
- Store thick wooden planks somewhere handy for use as walking boards to protect the soil structure.
- Mulch around fruit trees with rotted bark chippings.
- Keep removing cabbage white butterfly caterpillars from brassicas in mild weather.

VEG ON THE MENU

FRESH
Lettuce.
Spring onions.
Celeriac, Giant Prague.
Jerusalem artichoke.
Cauliflower.
Land cress.
Beetroot.
Carrot.
Leaf beet.
Swiss chard.
Leek.
Swede.
Scorzonera.
Brussels sprouts.
Salsify.

FROM STORE
Spuds, Kestrel and Cara.
Onions.
Garlic.
Chilli peppers.
Spaghetti squash.
Shallots.
Sunburst squash.

JOBS TO DO EACH WEEK

November, 3rd Week

In the Greenhouse
- Not much to do. Just keep an eye on plants.
- Ventilate daytime if not too cold.

On the Plot
- Winter-prune fruit trees.
- Bag-up and store wood ash from bonfires somewhere dry.
- Clear encroaching undergrowth where not wanted for wildlife habitat.
- Bag-up manure from local sources and store for later use.
- Check stored veg, reject anything that is not keeping well.
- Cut down globe artichoke crowns and mulch with leaf mould.
- Plant out corn salad plants.

VEG ON THE MENU

FRESH
Carrot.
Celeriac.
Beetroot.
Leek.
Salsify.

FROM STORE
Onions.
Spuds, Kestrel.
Garlic.
Red onions.
Butternut squash.

JOBS TO DO EACH WEEK

In the Greenhouse

- Enjoy the fact that there are no pressing jobs to do!

On the Plot

- Take time to enjoy the sights and sounds of the veg patch.
- Cut down and dig-in *Phacelia* green manure.
- Remove weeds where they are showing.
- Employ the hoe if it is dry.
- Trim hedges which border the plot, but leave others for wildlife until early February.

VEG ON THE MENU

FRESH
Parsnip.
Leaf beet.
Cauliflower.
Celeriac.
Beetroot.
Leek, Axima.
Swede.
Scorzonera.
Kale.
Brussels sprouts.
Jerusalem artichoke.

FROM STORE
Butternut squash.
Onions.
Spuds, Pink Fir Apple and Kestrel.
Red onions.
Chilli peppers.
Shallots.
Spaghetti squash.

JOBS TO DO EACH WEEK

In the Greenhouse

- Clean up dead and dying leaves from strawberry plants.
- Water strawberries.

On the Plot

- Do a bit of digging unless soil is sandy, in which case it is better to dig in the late winter / early spring.
- Sweep paths.
- Trim around the edges.
- Dig out leaf mould bin (from last year) and spread onto the plot.
- Turn the compost heap onto its head.

VEG ON THE MENU

FRESH
Celeriac.
Kale, Thousandhead.
Swede.
Leek, Axima.
Salsify.
Carrot.

FROM STORE
Onions.
Garlic.
Spuds, Kestrel.

JOBS TO DO EACH WEEK

In the Greenhouse

- Sow peas, Feltham First, in pots.
- Check on strawberry plants.
- Pot-on winter purslane.

On the Plot

- Clean and tidy the entrance to the greenhouse (remove trip hazards and potential accidents).
- Remove yellowing lower foliage from white sprouting broccoli.
- Tear off old, tough leaves from celeriac.
- Tend carrots still in the ground by checking for rot.
- Firm soil around brassicas.
- Order up seed catalogues for pleasant winter reading!

VEG ON THE MENU

FRESH

Celeriac.
Jerusalem artichoke.
Kale, Dwarf Green Curled and Thousandhead.
Brussels sprouts.
Leek, Axima.
Swede.

FROM STORE

Spaghetti squash.
Garlic.
Onions.
Spuds, Cara.
Shallots.

JOBS TO DO EACH WEEK

In the Greenhouse
- Not a lot to do so just relax and maybe check over equipment.

On the Plot
- Weed through Red Drumhead cabbages.
- Firm round red cabbages, then mulch with well-rotted manure.
- Weed as you harvest leeks.
- Mulch round brassicas with manure.
- Sort through shallots in store and select the firmest and best-looking for replanting around mid-winter.
- Prepare bed for shallots.
- Work out a planting plan for next year.

VEG ON THE MENU

FRESH
Leek, Axima.
Winter purslane.
Land cress.
Lettuce.
Spring onions.
Kale, Dwarf Green Curled, Thousandhead, Westland Winter.
Parsnip.
Swede.
Salsify.
Carrot.

FROM STORE
Onions.
Spuds.
Shallots.
Spaghetti squash.
Garlic.
Red onions.

JOBS TO DO EACH WEEK

In the Greenhouse

• Clean and disinfect pots and shelves if needs be but otherwise don't worry.

On the Plot

• Plant shallots.

VEG ON THE MENU

FRESH

Celeriac.
Leek.
Carrot.
Swede.
Salsify.
Scorzonera.
Kale.
Brussels sprouts.
Lettuce.
Parsnip.

FROM STORE

Onions.
Garlic.
Spuds, Pink Fir Apple.
Beetroot pickle.
Spaghetti squash.
Onion squash.
Shallots.

JOBS TO DO EACH WEEK

December, 4th Week

In the Greenhouse
• Clean and disinfect pots and shelves if needs be but otherwise don't worry.

On the Plot
• Plan next season's crop rotation on paper.
• Apply mulch of dry bracken to globe artichoke crowns.
• Harvest Brussels sprouts for feast-time.
• Pot up vine cuttings.
• Sort through squashes in store.

VEG ON THE MENU

FRESH
Leek, Axima.
Brussels sprouts.
Kale, Dwarf Green
Curled, Westland
Winter.
Celeriac.
Carrot, Autumn King.
Celeriac tops.
Jerusalem artichoke.
Leaf beet.
Spring onions.
Lettuce.
Winter purslanc.

FROM STORE
Spuds, Cara.
Garlic.
Onions.
Shallots.
Squash.

JOBS TO DO EACH WEEK

In the Greenhouse
- Water strawberries.
- Check over everything.
- Sieve leaf mould and sand to make potting compost.

On the Plot
- Prepare enclosed planting hole for fig tree against a south or south-west facing shed about 30 inches x 90 inches (76cm x 2.3 metres).
- Check all crops.
- Dig out stinging nettle and willowherb roots where not wanted.
- Clean yellowing leaves from kale.
- Compost marrows and squashes in store that are going off.
- Weed amongst Jerusalem artichokes.

VEG ON THE MENU

FRESH
Swiss chard.
Leaf beet.
Swede.
Leek.
Jerusalem artichoke.
Carrot.
Winter purslane.
Kale.
Cabbage, January King.
Brussels sprouts.

FROM STORE
Onions.
Garlic.
Spuds, Cara.

JOBS TO DO EACH WEEK

In the Greenhouse
- Remove yellowing leaves from strawberries.
- Set out seed potatoes to chit.
- Pot-on Winter Density lettuces.
- Sow tomatoes to raise in the house on a warm windowsill.

On the Plot
- Have a close-up look at catkins on cobnuts and filberts.
- Firm-in loosened shallots.
- Weed a plot for onions and fork-in compost.

VEG ON THE MENU

FRESH
Celeriac.
Winter purslane.
Brussels sprouts.
Cauliflower.
Carrot.
Parsnip.

FROM STORE
Spuds, Cara.
Shallots.
Onions.
Garlic.

JOBS TO DO EACH WEEK

In the Greenhouse
- Water seedlings.
- Check over.
- Cover chitting spuds with newspaper at night if temperatures threaten below freezing.
- Sow cabbages, Greyhound.
- Sow lettuce, Lobjoits Green Cos.

On the Plot
- Start to spread mature contents of the compost heap onto the garden.
- Tickle about here and there while harvesting.

VEG ON THE MENU

FRESH
Celeriac.
Jerusalem artichoke.
Leek.
Kale.
Cauliflower.
Cabbage, January King.
Scorzonera.
Corn salad.
Winter purslane.
Carrot.
Brussels sprouts.
Swiss chard.

FROM STORE
Garlic.
Onions.
Shallots.
Spuds, Pink Fir Apple and Cara.

JOBS TO DO EACH WEEK

In the Greenhouse
- Keep an eye on chitting spuds in extreme cold. Don't allow to get frost-bitten.
- Tend seedlings.

On the Plot
- Remove remains of sunflower stalks and remove to the compost heap.
- Plant garlic, Printador.
- Clear remaining leeks from main bed and heel-in near the house.
- Dig a trench for runner beans and start to fill with green kitchen waste.
- Transplant self-sown gooseberry from veg patch to wildlife bank at the back of the plot.
- Define plot edges by digging and weeding thoroughly.

VEG ON THE MENU

FRESH
Swede.
Cauliflower.
Cabbage, January King.
Parsnip.
Scorzonera.
Winter purslane.
Leek.
Celeriac.
Salsify.
Carrot.
Kale.
Brussels sprouts.

FROM STORE
Spuds, Cara.
Onions.
Garlic.
Shallots.

Veg on the Menu

APPLES

APPLES

Apple Upside-down Cake

Method:

1. Grease the sides, inside edges and base of an 8 inch (20cm) baking tray with margarine.

2. Peel and core 1 or 2 eating apples (enough to cover the tray base). Slice and blanche them.

3. Sprinkle light brown or muscovado sugar on top of the slices according to how sweet your tooth is. Fill all the gaps as well as putting enough to pat down on top of the apples.

4. Pour your favourite sponge-cake recipe over the sugar and apple mixture and bake as per your sponge recipe instructions.

5. When cooked, remove from the oven and allow to cool for 10 minutes. Use a knife to go round the edges to ensure nothing has stuck. Invert onto a cake plate.

6. Eat while still warm for maximum pleasure!

Apple Crumble

Ingredients:
- 3 lbs (1kg 350g) cooking apples such as Bramley Seedling
- 6 oz (175g) soft light brown sugar
- Pinch mixed spice
- Sprinkling ground almonds
- Dash of lemon juice (2 dashes even better!)
- Enough (but very little) water to avoid the apples sticking to pan. Could use undiluted orange squash instead.

Cook apples. When cold spread in a lightly greased casserole dish.

Crumble:
- 9 oz (250g) plain flour
- 6 oz (175g) margarine
- 3 oz (75g) caster sugar
- Dusting of dry porridge oats
- Optional: could also use ground almonds and/or ground hazelnuts in small quantities.

Method:

1. Sift the flour. Cut the margarine into small pieces and rub into the flour. Add sugar, any optional ingredients, and continue rubbing with your fingers until mixture clings together in large crumbs.

2. Cover apples with crumble, patting down slightly.

3. Cook at 200 degrees Centigrade (400 degrees Fahrenheit or Gas Mark 6) for 15 minutes then 190 degrees C (375 degrees F or Gas Mark 5) for a further 15 minutes until ready.

APPLES

Winter warming Apple-a-la-mode

Ingredients:
- 1 lb (450g) hard sweet eating apples (a variety that does not go fluffy when cooking, such as James Grieve, Egremont Russet or George Neal)
- 1 oz (25g) margarine
- 2 tablespoons caster sugar
- Sprinkling of ground almonds

Method:
Peel and thinly slice the apples.

Melt margarine in frying pan. Add sliced apples and sugar. Cook very gently until pale golden, sprinkle with ground almonds, turn over gently and cook for a further few minutes.

Serve hot with vanilla ice dessert.

BEANS, RUNNER OR FRENCH

Bean, Potato & Garlic Bhugia

Ingredients:
- Red chilli pod, fresh or dried
- Oil
- Jeera (ground cumin seeds)
- Garlic
- Beans
- Turmeric (haldi)
- Red chilli powder
- Salt
- Diced potatoes

Method:
1. Drizzle a generous dose of oil into a frying pan. Add 1 teaspoon cumin seeds, 2 teaspoons finely chopped garlic, broken red chilli pod complete with seeds. Fry briefly.
2. Add diced spuds and fry for 2 or 3 minutes turning frequently.
3. Add 1 teaspoon turmeric, 1 teaspoon red chilli powder, then chopped beans. Fry until spuds are cooked through on a low heat.

The term 'bhugia' means 'dry dish'. Serves best with boiled rice and a 'wet' lentil dish.

BEANS, RUNNER OR FRENCH

Beans with Baby Aubergines

Ingredients:

- Equal amounts of baby aubergines (rinsed, dried, stalks removed) and beans (chopped)
- Finger-nail sized pieces of fresh ginger, chopped
- 2 garlic cloves
- 1 onion, finely chopped
- 1 green chilli
- 3 ripe chopped tomatoes
- 1 teaspoon dried methi seeds
- Salt to taste
- Water and oil

Method:

1. Add peeled and chopped ginger and garlic to deseeded chilli. Add a drop of water and grind these ingredients into a paste.
2. Fry chopped onion until golden.
3. Add paste to the onions and fry for a further couple of minutes.
4. Combine with chopped beans and methi seeds, cooking for a further 10 minutes (keep an eye on it as extra water and / or oil may be needed to prevent sticking).
5. Cut aubergines into lengths, add to pan and cook for another 5 minutes.
6. Add chopped tomatoes and cook with a lid on at medium heat for a further 20 to 30 minutes until done.

BEETROOT

The joy of home-grown beetroot is that it is a 'double vegetable'. Although most folk only eat the plump and juicy root, the fresh and un-nibbled tops are a fantastic dish in their own right when cooked in the same manner as any other greens. Shop-bought beets are either missing the tops altogether or, if still intact, they are tired, drooping and not worth a second thought.

Boiled

Twist off the tops by hand. Cook beetroot in a lidded pot (40 minutes on a simmer after boil should suffice) or pressure cooker with a pinch of salt added to the water. If done in a pot, avoid the temptation to stick them with a fork to test whether they are done as each fork prick causes lovely red juices to run out.

When cool enough after cooking use your hands to simply 'pop' the beets out of their skins. They will shine like deep crimson marbles.

Nothing quite compares to the sight of steaming beets lavished with melting margarine oozing along the hot slices and meandering into the other items on the plate.

Pickled

Using sliced cooked beets and sliced raw onion, layer them alternately in a sterilised jar with beets at the bottom. When full add enough white or malt vinegar to cover. Put the lids on tightly and hide them away - out of sight and out of mind! Do not be tempted for at least a month. This pickle will easily last a year.

Grated Raw

Easy! Just grate a young beetroot into a bowl for a perfect accompaniment to baked potatoes.

BROAD BEANS

BROAD BEANS

Old broads need plenty of cooking and the skins are tough, so use young and tender beans for a truly wonderful culinary experience. A brief skirmish with a little boiling water in a pot for a couple of minutes should suffice.

In Salad

Cook and allow to cool; broad beans, asparagus and French beans.

Method:

Make a dressing of 1 tablespoon dried mustard powder, 2 tablespoons lemon juice, 5 tablespoons olive oil, salt and pepper to taste. Mix thoroughly and drizzle all over your three-veg dish.

Risotto

Ingredients:
- Cooked broad beans
- Diced carrots
- Finely chopped onions, shallots or leeks (can use all three)
- Olive oil
- Basmati rice
- Vegetable stock

Method:

1. Fry a combination of onions, shallots and / or leeks in a drop of olive oil until clear and / or tender.
2. Add the basmati rice and veg stock (1 cup of rice needs just over 1½ cups of stock).
3. Boil for 10 minutes, then allow to sit on an electric hob for a further 10 minutes. If gas, simmer for 20 minutes.
4. Add cooked broads and diced carrots for an attractive contrasting colour.
5. Toss and serve.

COURGETTES

COURGETTES

Courgettes with Onions

Ingredients:
• Oil
• 1 chopped medium white onion
• 3 chopped small courgettes (or 1 medium-sized) trimmed but not peeled
• Seasoning

Basically, the amount of courgette should be double that of the onion.

Method:
1. Fry onions in a drop of oil.
2. After only 1 or 2 minutes add chopped courgettes, then twist and shake of salt and pepper.
3. Cover pan and cook slowly to allow the moisture to come out of the courgettes.

Job done! This dish will always be sloppy but the amount of water in the dish may be reduced by frying hard at the end.

Lightly Spiced Courgettes

Ingredients:
• 2 lbs (900g) medium or small courgettes, trimmed but not peeled
• 1 large white onion, peeled and grated
• 2 cloves garlic, peeled and chopped
• ½ teaspoon cayenne pepper
• 1 teaspoon paprika
• ½ teaspoon freshly ground black pepper
• 1 teaspoon cumin seeds (or ground cumin, 'jeera' powder)
• Salt to taste
• 6 tablespoons olive oil
• 6 tablespoons water

Garnish: chopped flat-leaved parsley or chopped green coriander leaves plus lemon juice.

Method:
1. Combine onion, garlic, cayenne, paprika, black pepper, cumin and salt in a bowl. Add olive oil and water then mix well.
2. Cut courgette into strips and place in a large frying pan.
3. Pour the onion, herb and spice mixture over them.
4. Cover pan and cook over a medium heat for about 20 minutes or until courgettes are tender.

LEEKS

Shallow Fried

Chop across the leek to create circles. Use all the blanched white stalk and a reasonable portion of the green uppers ('flag').

Pan fry with a knob of margarine for 5 to 10 minutes, then season with salt and pepper and eat whilst hot.

Braised

1. Remove the topper-most portion of flag and cut leeks lengthways.
2. Place in an ovenproof dish, cover with stock, pinch of salt and twist of pepper.
3. Braise in the oven at 200 degrees C (400 degrees F or Gas Mark 6) for 45 minutes.

With Mustard

Cook exactly as for Braised Leeks, except do not cover with stock. Instead, lavish the leeks with French mustard before placing in the oven with a lid on.

ONIONS

Crispy Fried, as a garnish

1. Slice any amount of white onions very finely. Place in a frying pan with oil, cook very slowly until translucent. Sprinkle salt and a little bit of sugar on them before frying hard and hot. Be alert as they will go from a perfect lovely brown to a nasty burned black very suddenly. You can't afford to look away even once!
2. Lift pan immediately from the heat, scoop onions onto a flat dinner plate.
3. The onions will be 'sticky' so use a fork in each hand to separate the strands with a deft touch. Spread them thinly so that none are on top of each other. When cooled they will be beautifully crisp and crunchy.

Perfect as a garnish for fried rice.

Onion Rings

Roll sliced onions in a mixture of flour, chilli powder, salt and pepper. Fry and eat hot!

As a Sauce

Fry chopped onions with chopped tomatoes at approximately equal quantities. Add salt, pepper, ginger powder and fry slowly as the tomatoes take a while to cook to a mush.

When oil becomes speckled with red spots (a sure sign that the tomatoes have cooked) add some water, bring to the boil and serve on mashed potato, spaghetti or boiled cauliflower.

ONIONS

PARSNIP

Onion and Cauliflower Bhugia

Ingredients:
- Oil
- 1 onion sliced in rings
- 1 fresh or dried red chilli pod
- 1 cauliflower cut into florets
- Salt to taste
- 1 teaspoon cumin seeds
- 1 teaspoon sesame seeds
- 1 teaspoon fresh finely chopped ginger
- 1 chopped green chilli
- Fresh coriander leaves

Method:
1. Having fried the onion rings until pale, break red chilli pod into pieces over the onions and fry again.
2. Add cauliflower florets, ginger, green chilli and salt. Mix well, cover and cook on a low heat until the cauliflower is almost tender (stir occasionally to ensure even cooking).
3. Turn up the heat, add cumin and sesame seeds and stir briskly to get rid of any excess moisture.
4. Garnish with shredded coriander leaves (they must be well cut-up for their wonderful aroma to escape).

Roasted

1. Scrub parsnips to remove all the earth. If large, then slice in half lengthways. Place on a tray and drizzle olive oil all over them, add seasoning and toss well to thoroughly coat. Do this bit by hand if needs-be.
2. Roast in the oven at 200 degrees C (400 degrees F or Gas Mark 6) for 45 minutes, or until golden-brown, in tandem with onions, butternut squash, potatoes - a feast!
3. Add whole garlic cloves in their skins about 20 minutes from the end of cooking time.

PARSNIP

Soup

Ingredients:
- 2 or 3 medium sized parsnips
- 1 or 2 onions
- 1 potato
- Margarine
- Flour
- Seasoning
- Mixed herbs
- Bouquet garni

Method:
1. Soak chopped onions in melted margarine for 10 minutes.
2. Boil the chopped parsnips, save the water.
3. Fry the onions, add parsnips and parsnip water, add diced potato.
4. Sprinkle light dustings of flour into the mix if it needs thickening until the consistency is as you want it.
5. Add seasoning, herbs and bouquet garni.
6. Boil for half-an-hour, blend and serve.

Taste can be varied by using different combinations of herbs or spices.

Soup with Apple

As above but use less onion.

When boiling add one peeled and chopped cooking ('culinary') or eating ('dessert') apple.

POTATO

Salt and Pepper
1. Peel 4 medium potatoes and chop quite small.
2. Heat oil in a frying pan, add potatoes and 1 teaspoon ground black pepper. Fry hard. Add a small amount of water, fry hard again until the water disappears.
3. Add salt to taste, fry hard. Add a small amount of water, fry hard again until all water disappears. Potatoes should be cooked and ready to eat by then.

Wedges
1. Cut 6 large spuds (not peeled) lengthways into 8 wedges each. Place in icy water for 30 minutes.
2. Remove spuds from the water, dry them and toss in olive oil. Arrange skin-side down on an oiled baking tray.
3. Mix together 1 tablespoon dried oregano, 1 teaspoon black pepper, salt to taste. Sprinkle this mixture over the oiled spuds and bake at 200 degrees C (400 degrees F or Gas Mark 6) for 50 minutes until golden-brown.

Curried
1. Peel and boil 4 large spuds, then cut into lengths (or quarters if using medium sized).
2. While they are cooking, peel and finely chop 2 onions and 2 garlic cloves. Fry them in oil adding 2 teaspoons turmeric (haldi), 2 teaspoons red chilli powder and salt to taste. Fry until brown then add a dollop of tomato ketchup.
3. Throw away half the water from the boiled spuds. Add the above mixture to spuds with their remaining water. Stir in well and bring to the boil before turning off (the more water you leave with the spuds the more gravy you will have; half is about enough).

SHALLOTS

Roasted with Couscous

Roast a combination of veggies including shallots, garlic, chick peas and peppers in the oven until tender. Put them on a flat tray and drizzle with olive oil, adding salt and pepper to taste.

Remove from the oven and add to prepared couscous. Stir together to mix well and serve hot or cold.

SQUASH & PUMPKIN

Green Pumpkin Bhugia

Ingredients:
- Pumpkin (or squash), peeled and diced into small pieces
- 1 teaspoon cumin seeds
- Pinch dried methi (or ¼ teaspoon dried methi seeds)
- 1 teaspoon red chilli powder
- 1 teaspoon turmeric
- 1 teaspoon ground coriander (dhaniya)
- ½ teaspoon fennel seeds
- Salt
- ¼ teaspoon amchoor powder (dried ground mango)
- ⅛ teaspoon asafoetida powder (heeng)
- 1 tablespoon oil
- Sugar
- Fresh coriander

Method:
1. Heat oil, fry asafoetida first then immediately all the spices except amchoor powder.
2. Add the prepared pumpkin (or squash), cook slowly.
3. When pumpkin is cooked, after about 10 minutes, add amchoor powder plus a sprinkling of sugar.
4. Fry briefly and serve with finely chopped fresh coriander leaves.

SQUASH & PUMPKIN
SQUASH & PUMPKIN

Roasted Butternut

Method:

1. Slice butternut squash lengthways and then into quarters. Remove seeds and leave the skin on.
2. Place on a baking tray. Drizzle with olive oil, toss to coat. Add salt and pepper to taste.
3. Cook in oven at 200 degrees C (400 degrees F or Gas Mark 6) for 45 minutes.
4. Both the flesh and skin are edible and delicious.

Spicy Roasted

Use a winter squash (butternut or onion-type are especially good).

1. Make a mixture of 1 teaspoon each comprising ground coriander seeds and dried oregano, ½ teaspoon each of ground fennel seeds and black pepper, 1 teaspoon red chilli powder, pinch salt and 1 tablespoon of olive oil.
2. Cut squash lengthways and into quarters, remove seeds. Place on a baking tray, drizzle with olive oil and toss to coat.
3. Use fingers to apply the spice mixture to each piece of squash.
4. Roast at 200 degrees C (400 degrees F or gas Mark 6) for 45 minutes. Fresh squash means that the skin is easily edible so no scraping of flesh is required.

VARIOUS VEGGIES

VARIOUS VEGGIES

Summer Vegetable Pakoras

Ingredients:
- Gram flour, a sifted half-cup
- Turmeric, 1 teaspoon
- Chilli powder, 1 teaspoon
- Dhaniya powder (ground coriander seeds), 1½ teaspoon
- Salt to taste
- Heeng (ground asafoetida) - nicer if you have it but can do without. A pinch only to help with digestion as well as taste
- Dash or two of baking soda
- Plenty of oil
- Various vegetables including:
  - Very thinly sliced spuds
  - Florets of cauliflower
  - Florets of broccoli
  - Green beans
  - Single lettuce leaf
  - Single beet leaf or spinach
  - Chopped onion (if desired) mixed with chopped coriander and green chillies
  - Sliced aubergine (after salting and allowing moisture to come out)
  - Sliced courgettes

NOT peas, broad beans, corn off the cob as they cannot hold the batter.

Method:
Use enough gram flour for the amount of veg (start off with half a cup of flour) and blend together with all the spices, baking soda and water. Mix for a long time and beat it as if making a cake. This will allow the baking soda to work and make the mixture light and fluffy. It is easy to stop mixing too soon! The mixture needs to be thin enough to run off the vegetables yet thick enough for the batter to coat them before running off. The lightness and fluffiness helps to find this balance.

Heat 4 tablespoons of oil (to begin with, add more as and when required) in a frying pan. You can test the readiness of the oil by dropping a tiny drip of the gram flour mix into the oil. If it cooks (by going solid) right away then the oil is hot enough and ready.

Use various combinations of veg individually. Drag them through the batter and flop into the frying pan. Cook on medium to hot, ensuring that the oil cooks the veg through but does not burn gram flour coating before doing so. For leaves, cooking is virtually instantaneous. For florets, it is a bit longer.

GLOSSARY OF TERMS

ANNUAL (WEED): plant that completes its life cycle in one season.

ARABLE (FARMLAND): land used to grow crops.

BLANCH: in cooking, to plunge vegetables into boiling water to tenderise them and preserve their natural colour; in gardening, to exclude light to cause whiteness of produce.

BLIGHT: fungal disease affecting especially potatoes and tomatoes.

BLOSSOM-END ROT: sunken, brown flower-end of curcubits and tomatoes.

BRASSICA: any member of the cabbage tribe.

BROADCAST-SOW: scatter seeds by hand over an area as opposed to sowing in rows.

BUSH (APPLE): has an open centre branching from a trunk at about 2½ feet (75cm).

CATKIN (HAZEL): the male flowers that look like dangling lambs' tails.

CHIT (POTATOES): to set the individual spuds out so that shoots develop.

CHOKE (ARTICHOKE): the portion inside the bud which would develop into the petals.

CLAMP: method of storing veggies outdoors by covering with a mound of soil and straw to over-winter, or more simply with just soil.

CLOCHE: a clear covering for early and late veg protection which is portable.

COMPOST: an organic material made up principally of decomposed vegetable matter.

CROWN (ARTICHOKE, ASPARAGUS): base of the plant at ground level or just below.

CURCUBITS: cucumbers, squashes, marrows and courgettes.

DIRECT-SOWING: the act of sowing seeds straight into the ground as opposed to rearing seedlings in pots.

EARTH-UP: to draw soil up around the base of a plant, integral to potato cultivation but also applicable to leeks, celery, carrots and others.

EPHEMERAL (WEEDS): plants that produce numerous generations in a season.

FAN-TRAINED (MORELLO CHERRY OR OTHER FRUIT): to persuade a woody plant to grow flat against a fence or wall with branches spread as a fan.

FIRST-EARLY (POTATO): quick maturing variety of spud which is ready to dig in June.

FIRST THINNING: the initial act of removing excess seedlings and weaklings following sowing.

FLAG (LEEK): the leaves at the top of the plant.

FLORET: small flower head (of broccoli or cauliflower).

FORK-IN: using a garden fork to disturb and turn the soil surface.

FRIABLE SOIL: soil that is easily broken down into crumbs.

GARDENER'S SHUFFLE: small sideways steps taken forwards and backwards to firm a bed, principally before planting onion sets or brassicas.

GERMINATION: this is what happens when a seed first starts to develop into a plant.

GRAFT: the act of joining two separate parts of different plants together.

GREEN MANURE: a quick-growing cover crop grown to replenish nutrients and body in a soil, protect it, or both.

GREY MOULD (BOTRYTIS): grey or off-white fungal fuzz on crops, especially prone in a poorly ventilated greenhouse.

GROWBAG: plastic bag containing compost specially designed for the direct cultivation of a range of vegetables.

HALF-STANDARD (APPLE): one that has 3 to 5 feet (1 to 1.5 metres) of clear stem before branching occurs.

HARDEN OFF: the act of putting young crops from the greenhouse or windowsill outside during late-spring daytimes but bringing them under cover at night to acclimatise them.

HAULM (POTATO): the stems and leaves above ground (also used to describe similar in tomatoes).

HEEL-IN: to dig a rough hole or trench for short-term storage of bare-rooted trees, brassicas and leeks.

HONEYDEW: plant sap excreted by an aphid.

IN-THE-GREEN: term used to describe bulbous plants such as snowdrops when leaves are fully formed.

LEAF-MOULD: decomposed leaves used as a soil conditioner.

LEGUME: members of the pea and bean family with nitrogen-rich nodules on their roots.

LIQUID FERTILISER: concentrated liquid goodness which can be added to water for feeding crops, commonly made from nettles and comfrey.

MAIN-CROP: varieties of vegetables which produce the bulk of the crop in the main growing season.

MAINCROP (POTATO): spuds that mature over the course of the summer and are ready for digging from August onwards (blight permitting).

MULCH: protective layer of material placed on top of the soil and / or around plants to suppress weeds and conserve moisture.

MULTI-PURPOSE COMPOST: compost purchased in bags from the garden centre which suits any job from sowing seeds to raising crops in containers.

NOCTURNAL: active at night-time.

NURSERY BED: special area where crops are nurtured from the seedling stage until big enough to withstand life in the main bed.

PERENNIAL (WEED): one that comes back year after year from reserves stored in a fleshy or extensive root system.

PLANT-UP: to plant individual specimens into their final resting places, either on the plot or in grow-bags.

POT-ON / UP: to transfer seedlings into a bigger pot.

POTTING COMPOST: same as multi-purpose compost.

PRICKING-OUT: to carefully remove seedlings from a seed tray into individual pots.

ROOT-BALL: in container-grown plants, the knot of roots and growing medium in the pot or container.

ROOT NODULES: found on members of the pea and bean family, these distortions are home for nitrogen-fixing bacteria.

ROOTSTOCK: the part of a grafted plant (usually a fruit tree) which provides the roots.

ROSE (WATERING CAN): the fitting on the spout which filters water into a fine spray.

SALTING: the process of sprinkling salt onto veg to extract the moisture.

SCORCHING (OF LEAVES): happens when strong sunlight is magnified by water droplets on the leaf and it burns.

SECOND-EARLY (POTATO): early maturing variety ready to dig in July.

SEEDBED: ground prepared to a fine tilth for direct-sowing of seeds.

SEED-LEAVES: the initial pair of leaves which appear after germination.

SEEDLING: the name given to a plant in the early stages of growth.

SEED POTATO: usually certified disease-free, these individuals are the source of the potato crop and normally available in the shops from January (you can save your own, but there is a high disease risk).

SPEAR (ASPARAGUS): the much-prized and utterly delicious phallic shoot which is cut and eaten through late-April to early-June.

SPIT: in gardening terms, this is the length of a garden spade-head.

STANDARD (APPLE): a tree with about 6 feet (2 metres) of bare stem before branching.

STANDING CROPS: any crops which are ready to eat and are stored where they grew in the ground until harvest-time.

STATION-SOW: the act of sowing a few seeds together at regular intervals along a row as opposed to sowing thinly in a line.

STEP-OVER (APPLE): a variety grown on dwarfing rootstock as a single spread of two opposite branches trained horizontally about 12 inches (30 cm) above the ground.

SUCCESSION-SOWING: sowing varieties of veg at intervals, say fortnightly, to ensure a long cropping period.

SUMMER-PRUNE (APPLES & PEARS): cutting out woody stems to inhibit growth.

TASSEL (SWEETCORN): the female flower which forms as swollen tufts along the stalk.

TIE-IN: in fruit trees and tomatoes, the act of tying branches and stems to supports.

TILTH: of soil, the fine crumbly surface created by cultivation.

TOP-DRESS: to apply a material to the soil surface to replenish body or nutrients.

TOP-FRUIT: apples and pears.

TRANSLUCENT: almost see-through.

TUBER: a fleshy stem or root in which a plant stores reserves of food, usually underground.

UMBEL: a cluster of tiny flowers arising from the same point on stems the same length.

WIND-ROCK: damage caused by the wind, especially low down at the crown.

WINTER-PRUNE (APPLES & PEARS): cutting out dead, diseased and overcrowded branches to maintain an open centre to the tree and encourage growth.

INDEX